lynette jennings straight talk on decorating

Meredith® Books
Des Moines, Iowa

Meredith® Press
An imprint of Meredith® Books

Lynette Jennings. Straight Talk On Decorating
by Lynette Jennings

Executive Editor: Denise L. Caringer
Contributing Editor: Sharon Novotne O'Keefe
Art Director: Jerry J. Rank
Illustrations: Michael Burns
Copy Chief: Terri Fredrickson
Editorial Operations Manager: Karen Schirm
Managers, Book Production: Pam Kvitne, Marjorie J. Schenkelberg
Contributing Copy Editors: Jane Woychick
Contributing Proofreaders: Sue Fetters, Becky Danley,
    Susan Sanfrey
Indexer: Kathleen Poole
Electronic Production Coordinator: Paula Forest
Editorial and Design Assistants: Kaye Chabot, Mary Lee Gavin

Meredith® Books
Editor in Chief: James D. Blume
Design Director: Matt Strelecki
Managing Editor: Gregory H. Kayko

Director, Sales, Special Markets: Rita McMullen
Director, Sales, Premiums: Michael A. Peterson
Director, Sales, Retail: Tom Wierzbicki
Director, Book Marketing: Brad Elmitt
Director, Operations: George A. Susral
Director, Production: Douglas M. Johnston

Meredith Publishing Group
President, Publishing Group: Stephen M. Lacy

Meredith Corporation
Chairman and Chief Executive Officer: William T. Kerr

Chairman of the Executive Committee: E. T. Meredith III

All of us at Meredith® Books are dedicated to providing you with information and ideas to enhance your home. We welcome your comments and suggestions. Write to us at: Meredith Books, Home Decorating and Design Editorial Department, 1716 Locust St., Des Moines, IA 50309-3023.

If you would like to purchase any of our home decorating and design, cooking, crafts, gardening, or home improvement books, check wherever quality books are sold. Or visit us at: meredithbooks.com

contents

Decorating is your chance to show off the real you.

152   160   180   206   214   228   234

I'm with you...

Decorating your home is one of the hardest things you'll

IT'S NOT LIKE BUYING A CAR when, once you choose a make and model, they offer a few colors with the interiors already narrowed to a measly few. It may mean compromise, but at least it doesn't take too much time and angst before you choose from the six or so permutations and wind up with something of which you can be proud, at least for three years. And then the process repeats itself. NOW TAKE YOUR HOME. This is the largest, most obvious, hang-it-all-out-there demonstration of your personal taste. No matter what you do, EVERYONE YOU KNOW, EVER WILL KNOW, OR ARE RELATED TO BY BLOOD OR MARRIAGE WILL AT ONE TIME OR ANOTHER FIND THEIR WAY INTO YOUR DEEPEST COLOR, FURNITURE, AND WINDOW TREATMENT DESIRES AND PASS JUDGMENT. And, you'll have to live with your choices for years!

ever do in your domestic life.

Now you're in trouble. How much confidence do you have in your taste? Well, if you're normal—that is to say like most of the population in the Western hemisphere—you may rate it as 0 to 5 out of 10 at best.

UNLIKE BUYING A CAR, you pick a house out of hundreds of choices, all constructed in any one of a thousand variations of materials and colors. And that's only the exterior. Next comes the floor plan. Open space or a traditional montage of interconnected rooms? Which way do you prefer to live? And how can you know if you've only tried one of those options so far in your life?

Sooner or later, there's also the inevitable process of decorating, for which you may feel grossly inadequate. For one thing, too many media-made design gurus keep telling you "It's easy!" and "You can do it!" and "All you need is..." Ever wonder why *you're* having so much trouble if decorating is so simple? It's enough to make you wonder whether you're some kind of design illiterate. Well, you're not. Walk into any paint and wallpaper store, for example, and you can quickly see that decorating is anything but a casual choice-making process.

To complicate matters, there often is familial interference, two generations deep—design by a committee including parents who may profess "classics forever" and your children of speaking age who may roll their eyes at anything but MTV metallics.

As the pieces are finally coming together (if you've gotten that far), heaven help you if their completion or delivery gets out of sequence. If, say, the new draperies are hung but their upholstered mates won't arrive for weeks, you may end up having to defend an incomplete scheme.

Get it right in one room, and you've climbed Everest! That's the good news. The bad news? There are eight more rooms to go in the average American home. Then to add to the madness, they're all supposed to interconnect like a three-dimensional jigsaw puzzle.

Sigh. Peace be with you.

1

identity crisis

If you're like me, you often find yourself attracted to totally different styles. Uh-oh.

I'VE SPENT NEARLY **30** YEARS IN THE DESIGN BUSINESS, IN EVERY ASPECT OF IT from commercial installations, hotels, glamorous nightspots, restaurants, country cottages, chalets, and city lofts to suburban makeovers. Is decorating any easier for me? No. In fact it's worse. Misery of choice? Yes. The solution? Like you, I have to dig into why I'm attracted to many different ideas and looks. *The epitome of a design-lover's angst: One day I like the clean lines of Scandinavian simplicity; the next, it's cluttered Victorian!* When my husband is around I can see us in the woodsy lodge look, yet when I'm making choices for our Atlanta home, I go totally "Zen" austere. Sound familiar? I'm fortunate: I have two homes. The need to have a second house while I'm in production with my television show is a luxury that allows me to pamper both sides of my personality. **But like you,** I have to strip away everyone else's image of what my home should be before I can dig into **what I really want. Then** I have to figure out why I'm attracted to totally different styles. To complicate matters, I have to decide which style is right for my family and the way we *really* live. This is tough. Beginning in childhood we learn to evaluate ourselves, our tastes, and our status through the eyes of others. Isn't it time to change all that? For starters, forget what anyone else would say, and go with *your* gut as we look at the rooms on the next pages.

I call this easy elegance. I've always loved stripes—big ones. They're handsome. They give strength to a room like this, which could otherwise get too flowery for my taste. Yellow is always cheerful, especially when the shade is a light lemon, which won't mellow to a dingy look on an overcast day. One of my favorite ways to loosen a mood is with multiple patterns like these. Though the drapery, area rug, and needlepoint pillow share the same palette, creating a monochromatic scheme, they're different enough to allow for quick additions or subtractions of other accessories as they're collected. The sisal rug and sleek blinds contemporize the whole setting, which for me could otherwise feel a little stuffy. And yet I love the ornate collection of accessories. I admit, it's the luxury that I'm drawn to, and I can easily visualize myself "shlumphing" on the chair and ottoman in the foreground, in jeans and socks with the newspaper on a Saturday morning. Would my husband like it? He'd appreciate the artistry and sophistication, which would appeal to his academic side. Could he really live in it? No, it's much too studied for him. How about you?

when the indoors and outdoors connect this beautifully, you have harmony.

When I walked in, I was immediately drawn to the window. The immensity of the view was overwhelming. This is a fantastic example of the connection of architecture, decor, and livability with the setting. There is a completeness about it; because no single element stands out, the space exudes calm. Yet look closely: The room is upholstered in tapestries and damasks and tossed with woven silk throws and cushions. In a city house, those elements might seem darkly sophisticated. But balanced by the gutsy architecture and rugged view here, they send an invitation to kick off your shoes and get lost in the pillows by the fire. My husband and I both like this one. The scale suits him, and our overactive family could do no harm. It's elegant but livable.

Now this is a perfect example of a design dilemma—my husband and I like this too! We love the utter simplicity that contrasts with our complex lives. There's a certain peace about the room's lines. The sense of control feeds my perfectionism. The ballet of line and form is a feast for my eyes—perfect composition. I'm intrigued by the sense of humor the wavy partial canopy lends to the room. And I'm a collector of art craft, so the art plates caught my attention right away. My husband's fascination with Asian arts means he can get into this style too. But could we live in this look? To be honest, we're too messy. Disturb this with a briefcase dropped onto a chair, a basketball and backpack neglected under the table, and a stack of unread papers as a centerpiece and...? Well, you get the point. And yet I love this room. How about you?

design-lover's angst: I like this room too.

what I really love about this room is its freedom of color, its warmth and casualness.

Mentally try on this room for size. Wouldn't it look wonderful with the bed unmade, a robe tossed over the foot, and the morning newspaper scattered over the covers? This room is totally livable, with a gaiety that's infectious. Bedrooms should be the ultimate in comfort—kind of sleepy. I've always felt the best test of a bedroom is how you feel in it when you're under the weather. My husband and I both like this one.

Go back now and check your own reactions to these rooms. What works for you? What doesn't? If you have a spouse or partner, this is a good time to get his or her vote too. The only thing that counts is how you and your family feel.

attention skeptics

YES, I have a portfolio of hundreds of rooms, the history of my design practice. I've made many mistakes and learned from them. I've won awards and experimented with tools and materials befitting the finest wood shops and fabric studios. And in shooting my television show, I've seen see the most beautifully designed homes. So I should have it all perfected by now—a no-risk designer who's seen and done it all. Right? Oh, so very, very wrong! **The first lesson of design is that it is an art and not a science.** By definition, the process is unpredictable—a series of

decisions and adjustments as light and space come together. With every thread of imagination there is the potential for brilliance or more so-called mistakes. But what is a design mistake—this crisis that threatens to send your very being into the spiraling depths of furniture and fabric hell? A fluke of light you can't control? Color that shocks you out of your history with pastels? A table that seems too big? (Hint: Perhaps the table makes you uneasy simply because its scale is unfamiliar, not *wrong*.) I believe that the fear, **the frustration, and the nagging insecurity** that come with the process of decorating are derived from the preconception of photographable perfection. We pore over decorating magazines, clipping, ripping, filing dream home ideas. That's like living in the future instead of loving today. What's wrong with what you have now? Too small, too boring, not enough status, tired of the old look, furniture shabby? Or is it that you simply can't figure out what to do with your stuff and need something to jump-start your nesting libido? A little fresh inspiration, and you can *fall in love with your home all over again!*

I could tell you, "Loosen up," "Relax," "Work with what you have." But that's

unfair. It would be an oversimplification and would only elicit a sarcastic "Oh, sure. Not on my budget. I can't afford to redo it if I get it wrong. It has to be right the first time!" But what's "right"? Define "wrong." Maybe you're paralyzed by those "rules of decor" you learned in a high school art or home ec class. I can hear you: "What if I just hate it when I'm finished?" "What if everyone laughs at the color?" "What if I can't sell the house because I've unknowingly hurt its resale value?" Relax; here's where I can help.

Some say that you can't teach taste and that people are either born with an "eye" or not. I disagree! Design is *not* absolute. **Its beauty is in the eye of the beholder. We need to own up to who we are and what we like and then have the courage to live the way we want, with what we want.** Now that's design. **Taste is personal.** Period.

In this book, you will find rooms in a variety of decorative styles, color schemes, and uses of space. Some owners had design help; others followed their hearts. Don't use these as models to copy. **Look at these as imperfect rooms, adjusted and made livable based on personal preferences** and not necessarily on current trends. No room was

perfect to start with. Each has a design challenge that was met, awkward situations inherited with the architecture, furniture pieces that didn't "fit" or "go with." By the end of this, my first book, you will have come with me on a journey of discovering that **design has no hidden mysteries or agendas out of your reach.** It's only a word to describe the arrangement of a person's space, a series of adjustments and additions, a warm molding of elements to fit your personality like an old slipper—all to make your place feel like "home."

it's about freedom

OK, so you're free.
Now you have to think about what you
really, really want your home to be.
That's hard.

p.s. A porch that lives like the great indoors?
If your climate allows it, why not?

CHANCES ARE YOU AREN'T STARTING FROM SCRATCH. You've probably been collecting your furnishings and accessories since you left your parents' home: a mix of hand-me-downs, flea market treasures, memorable makeovers, good pieces you couldn't afford at the time but sprang for, current acquisitions, and maybe even artistic investments. Let's take a good look at what you have.

Get up right now and put a sticky note on everything that's simply not "you." If you have a partner, have him or her go through the same exercise. What have you never *really* liked?

You might now be thinking: "Whoa, this is getting dangerous. I can't afford to go where you're taking me. I have many things I don't like, but I didn't have a choice at the time and can't afford to do anything about it now." Wrong!

This isn't about money or buying everything new. Instead, it's about stepping away from design dictates to discover what your style really is without the confinements of outdated "shoulds" and "musts." **It's about saying "no" to stuff you don't like.**

NOW TRY THIS: Take away the labels from all the rooms in your house and look at each room strictly in terms of the amount and shape of the space, its view (and by the way, that can be a lake, a mountain, or just a tree or a flower pot), and the room's relationship to its adjacent space. How would you relabel each room? Forget for a minute about your furniture, because most of it has been typecast as well. Armoires, chests, chairs, and china cabinets can be used in any room in the house. **How you use them and what you store in them is only up to your imagination.**

So pick one room. Think about that space. Who says a living room has to be a living room? Do you really use it? When? With whom? How do other family members use the space? Does it have the best view or the biggest window in the house?

How do you spend most of your time at home? If, say, you're a writer and your partner is a crafter and most of your off time is spent at one of these activities, why relegate them to the basement? Of course if the activity is particularly messy, then the living room may not be practical, but how about using another ground floor room that also has a beautiful view?

If time is spent mostly with the kids, then why do so many family rooms wind up in the basement with no view or natural light? To contain the inevitable kids' clutter? So what? Why not live in the living room, kids' stuff and all? Are you saving the room and view for company? How often do guests come over, anyway? How much of that precious room-time is spent making an impression or conforming to the local neighborhood design or status expectations? Whoops! That hurt! Now I know that this exercise is a stretch. But how much will it hurt to be honest to yourself, your family, and your house? Here's a broad thought: When I consider the scenarios described above, I often wonder why the American house plan hasn't kept up with our varying cultural lifestyles. Instead too many of us seem to be squeezing our modern lives into homes designed for Victorian culture: parlors for receiving, living rooms for formal tea, dining rooms for formal serving, with the kitchen the domain of the cook and butler. Maybe this residential exploratory is extreme, but the point of the exercise is to awaken new and interesting possibilities for how you can *make your home conform to your needs.*

how do you really want to live?

Who says porches are only for sitting or dining? If you love summer nights and find the whir of crickets and cicadas music to your ears, why not turn your porch into a fair-weather bedroom?

Design at its best is all about freedom to make a house—mere "sticks and bricks"—into your "home," in all that that word has come to represent in your life and in the lives of your family. That sounds pretty heady. So what exactly does freedom mean in decorating? How about...

Freedom to interpret a space for a nontraditional use so you can use a room for what you'd like. That's what I did, and even for me it was frightening. Was I making decisions and expediting potentially expensive changes to the walls and floors that I would later regret or have to reverse to sell the house someday? No, common sense kept me—as it will keep you—on the right trail.

Freedom to live in your own era. Oh, now this is a touchy one. What's the difference between having the freedom of your era and being stuck in a bygone decade of passé trends—being, in other words, just plain old-fashioned? "Old" is a relative term. Old compared to what? The latest trend, yet to be proven and possibly passing? If done well and with commitment and quality, any and every design era is legitimate and respectable. After all, that's why many "old" trends come back over and over again. Good trends eventually become classics.

Freedom to make the well-loved tree in your front yard your primary view instead of obscuring the view with a "should" window treatment. Let go of old decorating provisos. Do you really have to treat absolutely every inch of glass area? Let's get back to the

Forget labels and use furnishings as you see fit. In this case, a suburban living room comes face-to-face with an old Victorian bedroom piece. Great idea! So what if the piece is labeled a wardrobe? Angled into a corner, it creates the room's perfect focal point—with storage to boot.

original purpose of window decoration: It's supposed to be a decorative method of controlling light and privacy. **But it seems to me that in many cases the decorative part of treating windows has overcome the practical purpose and subsequently the room.** When you walk into a room and your eye is immediately drawn to the window treatment, **you've lost control to a bolt of fabric.**

Freedom to play chess or do homework on the coffee table comfortably. I've lost track of the number of children's bedrooms that I have decorated, furnished, and accessorized to make the perfect play and homework spot. I could open a store with all the perfect desks, perfect lamps, and perfect chairs I've selected for making the inevitable and dreaded Sunday night homework—that opera of joy and angst—more pleasurable, private, efficient, quiet, motivational. I would have been better off buying a bigger coffee table or building a deeper, wider kitchen counter, complete with height-adjustable drafting chairs rather than barstools. In all these years of raising children (10 more years to go before homework becomes a grandmother's memory), the nightly homework ritual has never been performed in any location other than the busiest intersections of our house.

Freedom to make the living room into a poolroom. This is a tough one. Mind you, you won't get any argument from our teenage boys: "Hey, cool. Can my friends come every night after school?" And as for the girls who are old enough to realize the social advantages of early 8-ball training, our poolroom gives a whole new meaning to

Given their freedom, hutches, hunt boards, and breakfronts happily shed their "dining" labels. How about using them to stow and display your stuff in a den or bedroom? In this case, a reproduction Welsh dresser—a dining room classic—heads for the living room.

snookering unsuspecting quarry at the next Saturday night mixer. Believe me, as you will see from my once-upon-a-time living room in Chapter 3, this option works.

Freedom to paint the kitchen pink and the living room yellow, **ignoring the old 1940s rule of kitchens in yellow and girls' rooms in pink.** Those old precepts of proper color are still around. And what's worse is this business of colors that don't "GO." Just who are we going to blame for this one? Think about when you first heard those words. You were three, tearing out of your room after emptying the bottom drawers on the bedroom floor in search of one bottom and one top. Running to impress mom with your gymnastic prowess—your limbs equally divided into armholes and leg holes— you were met with a smile that faded to bewilderment and then to a knowing grin. "Honey, that's wonderful but it doesn't 'GO'!" Aghhhhhhhhh. That word! Who says? Look in your garden. Does one flower wilt because its bedmate doesn't "GO"? **Who declares these mismatches?** And why is it that the "rules" can only be broken by the published gurus of fashion runway extremes. Why is it OK for them and not for us? This toddler's scenario has been passed down through generations, the memory striking fear into the heart of every Saturday morning paint shopper. No wonder we're afraid of color. Blame your mother, and her mother, and her mother....

Close your eyes and picture this kitchen without the pale green, wide-striped walls. It would be blah, begging for something to add a little personality. Wallpaper? Sure, that could have been an option, but too many people choose a small-scale pattern. For a true transformation, make your color and pattern choices courageous ones. Later you will learn how to choose the right scale of pattern; for now remember that most are seen from a distance, primarily the other side of the room! Stripes are always in good taste. Stripes can be adapted to any period style or current trend. And the bigger the better, even in smaller rooms. As for the pale green, it's a garden color. It couldn't be more perfect for a food environment.

I am sure there are many more freedoms to be found as you identify rules you've never understood, followed blindly for lack of an alternative, and been afraid to break lest you make a costly and embarrassing "mistake."

Freedom is all about doing what you want, what feels right and looks good to your eye. But freedom isn't easy. FREEDOM IS SCARY. IT'S A BLANK CANVAS. It means you have to think about what you really, *really* want. That's hard.

Freedom is about finding your decorating "center." To do that, you have to face the truths about how you live in your home, how you interact with family and friends; those truths will suggest how to furnish and decorate your home. Compare what you have collected, arranged, and lived with against what you know in your heart and wallet is right for you. Easy to say. Hard to do. Definitely worth the effort.

And then there's purple. Truly one of the most intriguing colors in the spectrum, purple often is reserved for accents and bedrooms. It is a regal color that for many is addictive. No other color in the crayon box has such a loyal following. But for a kitchen? This beautiful picture answers the question. But just imagine standing in front of the paint center at the home improvement store this weekend and arriving at this color, this particular shade of orchid—an exquisite tint that transforms sunlight into the buttery complement of the cabinetry. Designer brilliance or pure chance? Can you actually imagine the result of a single color in a specific environment? No one knows for certain how a chosen color will look in a particular light, at different times of day, and in various seasons or weather conditions. Given that, how in the world can you make these decisions? GUTS.

take my home for instance

My husband's tastes are radically different from mine...and then we have the kids (and dog) to work into the equation. Now that's a challenge.

toronto: victorian+seven.

TAKE ONE FORMAL THREE-STORY VICTORIAN HOUSE WITH A TYPICAL 1900s FLOOR PLAN, A RABBIT WARREN OF SMALL, HIGH-CEILING ROOMS, AND MOVE IN A NEWLY BLENDED FAMILY OF SEVEN, ALL GETTING TO KNOW ONE ANOTHER OTHER, one another's friends, idiosyncrasies, habits, and attitudes, in the most erratic stages of their lives—preteen to teens. Got the picture? How could this house not be big enough?! Within weeks of moving in, it felt like an efficiency apartment. There was no way we could live in a traditional configuration and be happy. I took a good look at the reality of our lives—a snapshot of every day, every weekend—for a month. How was the time spent on weeknights? Saturday mornings, afternoons, and nights? Sundays and Sunday nights? How often did we really entertain? Who were our guests? I realized I'd had an image of my life that was more hopeful than real, more regimented than it really was—and add to that a new husband with an entirely different interpretation of elegance. His was casual and mine a ballet of line and form.

This required some major rethinking of our house and shook my professional experience to its roots. Whose rules had I been playing by all my adult designer life anyway? And why? IT'S OUR HOUSE. How dare the icons of style, these media-made gurus of color, these dictators of snobbery tell me how I should live in my home!

Welcome to our house. This is the main intersection, where the entry, stairs, living room/poolroom, and the room used for dining, lounging, and homework converge. There's no area rug to get wrinkled and no furniture to collect dropped stuff. Those were strategic decisions. At Christmas, there's a tree in place of the old pine saw-toothed cabinet. Most of the year, this space serves as the practice hall for flute, trumpet, violin, or clarinet, depending on whose gig is up next. With no fabrics to absorb sounds, the space echoes—and that's just how our budding musicians like it.

this table is the heart

# of our home.

The main event, the heart of our home is this two-generations-old table that originally belonged to my husband's family. It's an awkwardly narrow and round-ended 92-inch table, heavily scarred and split, but it continues to be loved—and will be into a future generation, I'm sure.

I had no idea how much even I had been influenced by my own design industry. Such incredible pressure, I thought. What "rules" have I bought into?! Suddenly, I had a whole new appreciation and sympathy for what you must go through every time you make a room-related decision.

If our exposed brick-and-rubble wall looks a little unfinished—well, it is. On purpose. When we added an office to the rear of the house, we broke through the existing rear structure, exposing a double brick wall of yellow interior and red exterior. There's something about an unfinished wall that reaches into my soul. My husband was intrigued with what I could do to integrate it with the adjacent formal walls. The kids thought it looked "weird." There is actually a design industry word for it—"deconstructionist." This term describes the eclectic mix of opposites: crude rustic texture against formal traditional finishes. The accessories and art double the impression: a large unframed work of the North Country pitted against the gilt-framed island woman and the black-and-brass reading lamp, a primitive yard table in the corner flanked by French armchairs clad in silk tapestry.

But my children have their own theory. They would tell you that the reason I don't like things to look too finished is that once a place is done I will want to move again and start another renovation. As much as they've always found the new projects exciting, they're just as happy explaining the unfinished walls to their friends, confident that they won't be packing for a while.

Here's a warming trend that's perfect for our cool Canadian climate—layer on the textures, mixing the rugged with the refined. Rough walls, aged woods, woven tapestry fabric, nubby rugs—and, yes, fuzzy dog!—make cozy companions in a corner of our Toronto dining/sitting room.

this is action central—
the most traveled path.

My husband and I both love to cook, so we needed space. The island is 4 feet deep—and for me still not enough counter space! Although you can't tell from this picture, the lower cabinets on either side of the stove were installed 6 inches out from the walls to make space for extra-deep countertops. This is not a kitchen with appliances neatly tucked into rolltop garages. We use everything too frequently. It approaches a restaurant kitchen and with good reason: With five children and their friends circling the fridge, microwave oven, and pantry, the stove is rarely cool and crumbs rarely swept.

remember, design is about life.
With five kids, a sandwich corner
was a must.

The sandwich corner: Bread is the largest commodity with a family of this size. A bread basket 30 inches wide barely carries enough loaves for a couple of days. Deep counters are a must. I'm not crazy about upper cabinets; they're tough for kids to reach. So a full-height pantry 30 inches deep stores all staples, serving dishes, and a full baking center. This is the most important storage feature in our kitchen. Dishes, pots, lids, and plastic storage all go in deep drawers with industrial-strength glides.

ABOVE: OK, so I had to be a little different. Truth is, I couldn't make up my mind on hardware—so many interesting shapes and forms. But there also was a practical reason. Try telling someone where to find something in your kitchen. For us, the cereal is behind the leaf door, and the zippered plastic bags behind the chili-pepper door! And as for placement—well, that's just designer license.

OPPOSITE: The drink corner: A professional milkshake maker, complete with stainless-steel shakers and monstrous glassware, was my Christmas gift to the family one year.

feel free to interpret a space for a nontraditional role.

No living room? That's right. The kids and their friends love this. Even when we entertain formally, bathing the entire area in candlelight, it seems that everyone still wants to shoot a little pool, hang around the kitchen counter, and sit at the table with a glass of wine. We love it that way.

a modern muse in atlanta.

WALK IN THROUGH THE FRONT DOOR OF OUR SOUTHERN HOME AND YOU'RE DRAWN TO THE WOODED HILLS BEYOND THE REAR GLASS WALL. This house—my home when I'm in production on my television show—is a 20th-century-style glass box hanging on a wooded hillside. The interior is a play of light and sculpted two-story walls, an intersection of slabs and shadows. The box is punctured through its middle with a slit of skylights that runs the full width of the house, scattering light down through three floors of staircase.

The shape of the house is pure architecture of the 1950s and 1960s—a classic period rooted in the Bauhaus school. And white is the authentic color of that particular look. So as not to disturb the home's integrity, and as much as I profess color, I've combined the woodland scene, with its daily changes, with a simple palette of naturals in the furnishings to create a delicate, texturally rich scheme.

Restrained design and neutral hues enhance the interplay between orderly modern architecture and the wild tangle of trees just outside. Showcased against gallery-white walls and polished floors, every object, from the grand piano to a grandly scaled floor plant, assumes a sculptural stance.

with few furnishings and little clutter, this home gives my imagination room to roam. The absence of furniture could be disturbing to some. To me, however, this is a pregnant space. It makes room for you and your imagination. And more practically, it makes room for the kids to dance, horse around, build projects, and just be kids.

the ultimate visual peace.

For me, the lack of "stuff" creates the ultimate visual peace. My husband has a bit of "Zen" in his soul. He loves the simplicity—but even more the uninterrupted communion with the wooded vistas through a home that is mostly glass.

establish your style with the things that you love.

My husband's primitive boat model, the contemporary sofa-chairs, and the 17th-century French gilded mirror reflect my leanings toward eclecticism. Different in styles and origins, the items are linked by their grand scale.

ABOVE: Again, the counterpoint shows up—this time in the dining room. An S-curved wall becomes sculpture, its shape enhanced by two incongruous compositions: a grouping of wood spoons on one side, and around the curve a marriage of a copper cone and a stick ladder. The austere environment draws attention to the shapes and textures of such simple, primitive objects, elevating them to the status of art.

OPPOSITE: One of the most interesting design elements in our glass house is the level of the dining room windows. When you are standing, the windows seem unusually low, almost forcing you to be seated. Sit down, and the panes are perfectly positioned to showcase the wooded valley and stream.

ABOVE LEFT: Tiny kitchen, room for one, but it's one of my favorite spaces. When we're all together in Atlanta, the kitchen is still the center point. And it's amazing how the smaller space is irrelevant. Stacking our china in a modern version of a country-style open-cupboard arrangement gives it that accessibility that we so love in our northern house—everything is at fingertip reach. And of course, to make it artistic, we've stocked it with a random, unmatched collection of all-white dishware.

ABOVE RIGHT: Not an inch was wasted in the construction of this house. The underside of the staircase to the second floor telescopes through to an odd bulkhead over the cooktop. Add the boxed hood vent, and the upper cupboard becomes an asymmetrical sculpture. The white ceramic boxes are old battery molds—and who would guess? They make great hiding places for chocolate!

OPPOSITE: In a niche flanked by two glass walls, a wall of storage and a simple outdoor table with a stone inset create a highly serviceable dining spot that's elegant in its simplicity. It's one of our favorite places for a quiet breakfast—and tea with the squirrels.

4

the scary part
Relax!
Decorating is fun when you take away the fear and the rules.

THIS IS THE HARDEST PART OF THIS BOOK: GETTING YOU TO IDENTIFY WHAT IT IS ABOUT YOUR HOME, A ROOM, A CORNER, OR EVEN THE EXTERIOR PLOT that makes you unhappy or uncomfortable. **Getting to the root is the first step.** And that's difficult when you've invested emotionally and financially in certain ingredients—furniture, accessories, and even color and pattern. Maybe you've even bought the wrong house? You're now totally dissatisfied with what you have? *"Thanks, Lynette. Now, I'm really miserable."* Take it easy. The answers are within you.

I wish I could personally answer the thousands of letters I receive weekly about this step-by-step process of getting to the root of a design problem. You see, because the beauty of design is in the eye of the beholder, what is unsatisfactory to you may be fine for someone else. In order for me or any designer to offer remedies, you need to be able to describe your dissatisfaction. Once you become aware of what it is you don't like, you can choose from several solutions that will be right for *your* eye and *your* comfort level. A designer is only there to offer alternatives. It's *your* house! **Decorating is fun when you take away the fear and rules and develop confidence in your own decision-making ability.** After all, this whole process is meant to help you discover your personal style—even if you aren't sure you have one, or you've been living in someone else's style by accident, or (the worst sin of all) you've been ignoring your own good sensibilities and simply copycatting.

"Style" refers to the way that you respond to, interpret, and, in a broad sense, go through life. You've heard people say that certain stars and celebrities, or even people around you, have a great sense of style. It's usually in reference to how they dress, what they drive, where they dine, or just how they interact with others. And of course, that phrasing is used in the description of their homes. This puts them in a category: They're "in," sometimes at the expense of slotting you and others in the "out" box. What is it that makes what they do so different? Most of the time it has nothing to do with what the fashion judges say is trendy. It's 100 percent about confidence. That means execution with conviction. Real style means being sure of who you are, how you want to live, and what you want for your loved ones and going for it in the face of the influences of your peers and the media.

How do you get there—especially when it comes to improving your home? Get those sticky-notes going. First, analyze what you already have and make a list of your dreams. Now let's put the information together and get started.

terrified of color?

IT'S PRETTY TYPICAL IN A DECORATING BOOK TO START THE LEARNING PROCESS WITH A GLOSSARY OF STYLES: country, traditional, modern, Mediterranean, up-country, the lodge look, French, Tuscan, Scandinavian, and so on. And each description would be accompanied by a line drawing of a chair and a photograph of a room representing the quintessential style specimen.

You would probably be asked to choose a category that best describes your home; this is supposed to help you identify your personal and existing style. But unless the decorator has just left, in which case you probably wouldn't be reading this book, you would most likely respond with a discouraged sigh: "I don't have a style" or "My things don't look anything like any of this and probably never will; I must be so far out of the game that I may as well quit now." Or you might take a look around the house and drop everything into one of two boxes: traditional/country (either formal or casual) or contemporary/modern (kind of sleek and trendy—Pier 1, IKEA, Crate&Barrel). So let's not go there.

...a little color here?

...a lot of color everywhere? you decide.

Let's start with color. Color holds the possibility of solving the majority of design problems. **Color affects space. Color reorders the priority of features and elements in a room.** Color can make a room livable. However, color remains the biggest stumbling block, regardless of the historical significance of your furniture and regardless of personal style, budget, size of home, architectural challenges, or the environmental context. In other words, color is the design element that stumps nearly everyone—celebrity or not. *And yet, color is essential. It is the element that makes a house a home.* Color is what makes you, your furniture, collectibles, art, posters, your grandmother's bedspread, your first macramé, your Austrian crystal lamp, your daughter's first finger painting, your husband's tattered chair, your silk settee all look wonderful!

fall in love with your home.
NO MATTER HOW PRACTICAL YOU MIGHT THINK YOU ARE, YOUR RELATIONSHIP WITH YOUR HOME IS AN EMOTIONAL ONE. Ask a real estate agent what the most common exclamation is when clients first walk into the house that they end up buying: "Oh, I love it!" Bingo. That's the most common response—and it's an emotional one. There it is.

Color affects how you feel about your home, a room, a corner. Color determines the mood that those spaces evoke from within your psyche at any given time. When you feel sad, where do you go in your home? What chair do you sit in? What lights do you have on or off? Which window do you stare out of? When you're elated, where do you go? Which are the happy places—where are they now and where *could* they be if you simply splashed on some fresh color?

Here's a great example of color confidence. I love the way the yellow plays off the orange, turning a potentially dull hallway into a spot that evokes a smile. See how the white wall acts like a mat to frame the orange niche? Wonderful! (Hmmm...what could you do with a can of paint?)

What a great lesson in changing the feeling of a country-style dining room. Same furniture, fresh style! White woodwork frames purple walls for graphic punch, a modern approach enhanced by the bold artwork. Instead of the expected chandelier, adjustable halogen lights add function—and fun—overhead.

where are your happy places?

You know that certain areas of your home allow you to cruise through the blues, snap you out of your funk, or even encourage you to dance a jig. That's why you have a preference for certain colors. They make you happy, mellow, calm, energetic, even hungry. You may not have consciously thought of the effects of colors as you chose them but rather made a passive decision based on your personal experience with them: A sentimental memory of a room from your childhood, a relationship with your wardrobe, or even an inspiration from an artifact or the garden can inspire a palette.

I have asked hundreds of people why, given the power of color, they insist on living with off-whites and neutrals. From the look of their clothing, they aren't opposed to color. I hope that they are only afraid of choosing the wrong color and therefore opt for none at all. But even when under the guidance of a professional, most people will select a neutral or pastel palette. At the same time, those same people may covet a colorful home, drool over decorator magazines showcasing colorful rooms, and even spend hours in front of a display of 3,500 paint chips and still walk out of the store with off-white. Fear? *Usually.* But of what? Walk into a house filled with yellows, medium blues, greens, and corals, all brightened with white trim, and you will remember it as a "happy" house. Can you get the blues in a brilliant yellow room? Can you be riotously celebratory in a gray, black, and eggplant room? There's no right or wrong answer here—it's very personal. So stick to your instincts, don't be afraid of the result, and don't fall into measuring your natural selections against what appear to be the commandments of design.

I have to smile when I see this picture. Who says a formal dining room can't be lighthearted too? The colorful, casually placed pots of flowers carry out the bright mood set by the colorful artwork and walls. (Come on now; aren't you just a little bored with your own bland walls?)

just think...there are no right or wrong answers.

color is simply personal.

Classic modern furnishings, white built-ins, wood floor—OK so far. But the owner went a step further and painted one wall a bold color and added bright birdhouses and rooster prints. In this context, even a lineup of Granny Smith apples can show off its snappy hue. (You can eat the "artwork!" Today, it's apples. Tomorrow? How about oranges?) Why this aqua wall? Why not? Would yellow have worked too? Sure. Remember—this is *personal*.

5

"my room is too small"

and other feeble excuses.
There's no excuse for not putting a little color
into your life.
Small space? Rainy climate?
Your spouse hates color?
Nah. I'm not buying it.

IN EVERY LIVE APPEARANCE I'VE MADE ANYWHERE IN NORTH AMERICA, FROM PORTLAND TO AUSTIN TO NEW ORLEANS TO CHICAGO TO TORONTO TO ORLANDO, I have opened by asking the audience: "How many of you still have white or off-white walls?" And in every instance, more than three-fourths of the hands go up—slowly, tentatively, with shy giggles, only to be withdrawn quickly, embarrassed. Why?

Unlike a failed crafts project that can be shoved into the closet, decorating with color means wearing your taste on your sleeve—subject to scrutiny by all. Even your dearly beloved might roll his or her eyes with, "Whatever you like, honey." Your peer-approval-driven children also may roll their eyes with simply the "Whatever!" part of that phrase, mumbling about never bringing their friends home again.

When you've chosen a beige neutral carpet so that it goes with everything, a beige sofa because it goes with everything, an off-white wall to go with everything, and no evidence of that marvelous "everything" is anywhere to be seen—well, I rest my case. And then there are the many common excuses for colorless rooms:

(*Check the one that best fits you.*)

- [ ] **myth#1** It rains too much in our city; the skies often are gray, so I need white.
- [ ] myth#2 My room is too small; color will make it appear smaller yet.
- [ ] myth#3 My windows are too small; there's not enough light for color.
- [ ] **myth#4** My spouse hates color, so I'm stuck in neutral.
- [ ] **myth#5** My furniture is too dark; I need white to lighten the room.
- [ ] myth#6 My home has an open floor plan, so I have to use the same color scheme throughout the house.
- [ ] myth#7 I don't know where to start, so it's best to do nothing.
- [ ] **myth#8** My room faces west. Won't warm colors make the room feel hot?
- [ ] myth#9 My real estate agent says white rooms sell houses; color may hurt my home's resale value.

If I've missed any of your own "I can't have color" myths, write to me. These are serious issues! The fear of risk is positively palpable! The entire country is compromised into visual sterility! The future seems bleak...and beige!

DISCLAIMER! If you positively love white down to your soul, if you've used off-white as a true color, mixed with softened, elegant, delicate hues and balanced with Zen shapes and austere placements of studied, deliberately placed artifacts, then you're okay. But if your "builder whites" are simply stopgaps until you summon the courage to paint or hire a decorator at an hourly rate, please, please, please read on.

Let me crush the previously listed myths, one at a time. Read on so you can feel free to *color your home your way*—at last.

myth#1 "It rains too much in our city; the skies are often gray, so I need white."

Reality: White is not going to make it better. The blue-gray color of the sky will reflect in the white, resulting in a drab blue-gray environment, which is exactly what you *don't* want! Clean, clear, bright colors would be very much better. They don't have to be saturated and vivid; TRY MEDIUM STRENGTHS OF CRISP PRIMARY COLORS IF YOU'RE A TAD TIMID. White trim can brighten a color in this context. Take a lesson from the paint manufacturers who display their color chips on a stark white background. A creamy edge on a color diminishes the brilliance. A white border sharpens it. Look how crisp the colors below appear because they are framed in white.

myth#2 "My room is too small; color will make it appear smaller yet."

Reality: Color is not going to make a big difference. We once conducted an experiment by building two identical rooms—mirror images of each other, complete with the same furnishings and accessories placed in exactly the same configuration. The only difference was that one was painted off-white and the other a medium-dark sage green. We marched a large number of people through these rooms and conducted a focus group afterward. We asked if they thought the sage green room was the same size or smaller, and if smaller, by how much? The overwhelming majority didn't notice size at all; a few felt the room might be smaller, but by no more than 6 inches. The attitude was that they liked the green room, so its size didn't matter. By comparison, the off-white room felt cold and naked. *Now, are you sacrificing style, personality, mood, and elegance to gain an illusion of 6 inches of extra space? Is it worth it?*

When you see a beautiful room in a magazine layout, when you visit a friend's home that has been beautifully decorated or wander through a gorgeous model suite or designer showcase house, do you ever ask how large a room is? No. And, even more important, does its size matter, anyway, if you really love the room? No, because you love the room. There's that word again. Love. Emotion. IT'S BETTER TO HAVE A GORGEOUS, COMFORTABLE ROOM FULL OF COLORFUL PERSONALITY THAN A WHITE BOX.

Turn to the simple guest room on page 84. It isn't fancy, and it's not a priority for furniture spending. But it is elegant and tasteful, evoking a calm, peaceful mood. Imagine it in an "un-color." With off-white walls, it would have been completely drab, sending the message that the room was an afterthought and that guests are not important. In fact you would have to work much harder at decorating it, with better furniture and more accessories, to bring its personality up to a comfortable level. In this case, a gallon of interesting color did it all and for much less money. Notice the bright white trim around the natural wood door. The white brightens up the wall color and showcases the old doors as decorative elements.

OK, so if you really are a "beige" person, how can you give your rooms a little oomph? First, understand that off-whites and beiges are true colors. When you see beige on a stark white color chip at the paint store, your impression is that the color is strong enough for your room. But when you roll that same beige on the walls of a sunlit room, it pales to nearly white. What then? Painting the trim stark white will help enormously, creating the same effect as on the paint chip and rendering the beige as a color rather than an "un-color." Take a cue from these other scenarios.

How dull would this room be without its restful sage green walls? The color adds warmth with little effect on the room's apparent size.

Challenge: Is there a simple way to make a small home seem bigger?

Solution: *Paint adjacent rooms the same color, and walls seem to disappear, enhancing visual flow from one space to another to create spaciousness.*

Are you a "beige" person? Neutral fabrics? Natural medium to light wood furniture? That's fine as long as you create color contrast to bring your favorite things forward and to give a room balance, scale, and definition. Place a beige sofa in front of a beige wall or a yellow sofa in front of a yellow wall, and the sofas disappear. When you paint the wall in a deeper shade or a lighter tint of the same color, you create contrast. The deeper the contrast, the more pronounced the sofa will be. Notice I didn't say that the darker wall will be more pronounced! That's what most are afraid of—that the colored walls will take over. It's the opposite that occurs. The deeper the walls and the more vivid the color, the

ABOVE LEFT AND RIGHT: A small home gains an expansive look when adjoining rooms share the same wall color.

more important your furniture and accessories become. The walls are the backdrop to your stage. They present the main act. In the first of the pictures on this page, everything is neutralized. In the second, you can see how much more you notice the stripe in the sofa fabric. Even the detail in the photograph is more pronounced.

Challenge: **I'm a "beige" person. I love neutrals. How can I make my room more interesting, more professional looking?**

Solution: *Instead of a light beige, deepen the color on your walls to at least a mid-tone for a look of confidence—and drama!*

Let's take the neutral scheme further. In the room opposite the contrast between the mid-tone beige on the walls and the lighter upholstery brings the sofa forward. Though the cushions are neutral, they pick up various shades of the wall color and

ABOVE LEFT AND RIGHT: There's nothing wrong with this room, but look how much more interesting things become and how much stronger the chair's stripes appear when the wall is painted a darker shade. OPPOSITE: Fresh paint wakes up the light upholstery in this living room too.

play with the scale. The pine furniture is also classified as neutral. Now place one hand over the red-clothed table at the far left of the photo and the other hand over the petit-point area rug. All beige. Even though the contrast between walls and furnishings is an improvement, we haven't really solved your fear of color.

Challenge: **My room is all neutral. I'm so used to it that I don't know what color to choose to brighten it (or even where to put the color).**

Solution: *Chances are you chose neutrals because they go with everything and every color. Now let's get you going by choosing that "every" color! Don't get hung up searching for the perfect shade of something; it's not that complicated. Start with the six colors in a basic crayon box—red, yellow, orange, blue, purple, green. Choose your favorite and buy one large but inexpensive item in that color. Place it, live with it, and every time you walk into that room, you will smile—and gain color confidence!*

The picture opposite shows one of my favorite color schemes. I love this wall color. My office and several rooms in my home are "stone" colored. My taste runs to the eclectic. I love bringing in new things—flowers, pillows in different colors depending on the day or season—so I hate being boxed into a specific scheme. I agree that neutrals go with everything. I must admit that I'm a bit of a "beige" person too, because of the flexibility beige allows. But to keep things interesting, I opt for dark versions of neutrals on the walls to highlight furniture, textures, and minute details of accessories. The texture of these chairs opposite would die against a pale wall. It's the depth of the background that brings your eye to the detail in the doors of the hall table, the delicacy of the floral elements, and the rough texture of the chairs.

Yes, small spaces can have big color. I admit that I like neutrals myself—but only when they have some real guts to them. Instead of the flatness of a light beige or taupe wall, this darker neutral adds depth to the room by allowing the light furnishings to pop out against it.

myth#3 "My windows are too small; there's not enough light for color."

Reality: If the windows are that small, then they don't matter, anyway, so why let them dictate your color scheme? The bit of light you're getting from them isn't going to make a big impact on your room even if your walls are white, so go ahead and paint your walls the color you really want.

The bathroom shown here is approximately 5×8 feet—a standard size. The window is shaped, deep set, and tiny. It is useless as a light source. Decorating this

ABOVE: A small bath gets warmth and elegance from rich, earth-hued walls. OPPOSITE: Boring white walls will not do much to enhance the natural light that's provided by one small or mid-size window. Instead, roll on some color to energize the room with fresh style—and drama!

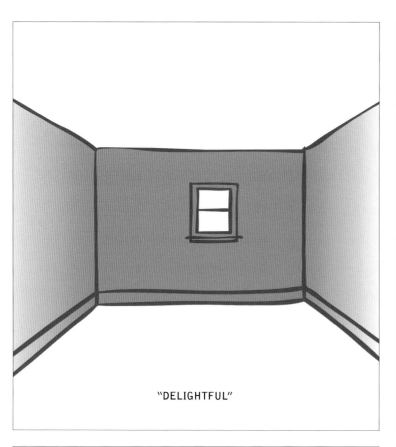

"DELIGHTFUL"

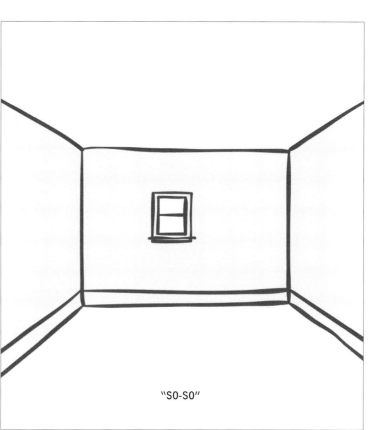

"SO-SO"

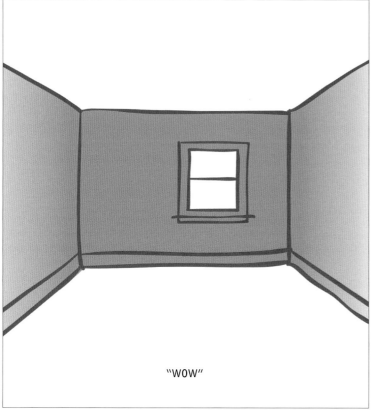

"WOW"

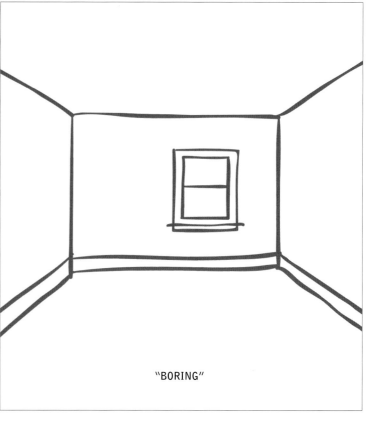

"BORING"

bathroom to make use of its natural light would have been futile—and a terrible waste of a decorating opportunity. *Rich color is soothing, handsome, exciting, exotic, and actually very easy to decorate around.* The best thing to happen to this small bathroom was the wall of mirror behind the vanity. That mirror does far more to expand the room's apparent size than white walls ever could have done. And the little window, left untreated, becomes a decorative feature like a painting or sculpture.

Challenge: **My window is small and looks onto the house next door, so I need some kind of window treatment. A colorful window treatment will block the light and call attention to the tiny window, so I'm stuck with beige or white.**

Solution: *Ignore the window. If it doesn't provide enough light to make a difference, why compromise the room's decor? Turn the room into a rich and elegant jewel box with painted walls, then blend the window into the walls with matching draperies or blinds.*

myth#4 "My spouse hates color, so I'm stuck in neutral."

Reality: It's rare that someone really dislikes color. Your spouse may be afraid of color, uneasy with your color preferences, worried about the domino effect of committing to more color in other rooms, or feeling a little out of control because he or she can't quite picture the end result or the effect the wall color may have on favorite possessions. Communication is key here. If your spouse is nervous, go easy. Maybe your spouse lived in too many white apartments, grew up with pale pastels, or simply got stuck in a color rut.

MY ADVICE: Choose color together. Compromise by introducing color to a powder

White trim shows off a mellow wall color that's echoed in the rug and fabrics. The subtle surprise? Rich red paint on the wall behind the open shelves.

Most people are comfortable decorating with the hues they wear. If your spouse is "stuck in neutrals," check the closet for colorful inspiration.

room, den, or extra bedroom first. Choose medium natural shades, such as soft camel, wedgwood blue, sage green. Avoid the darker and brighter shades until your mate develops a bigger appetite for color.

The most successful schemes I have found are developed from a person's wardrobe. Look in the closet. Is your mate a "brown/burgundy" person? Taupes and sage greens? Navy and brights? Most people are more comfortable using the colors they wear as colors for their home. In the photo above, I have matched color chips to a brown group and a green group. These are handsome, architectural, all based on a natural palette. Add punch with accessories.

myth#5 "My furniture is too dark; I need white to lighten the room."

Reality: Surrounding dark or large, bulky wood furniture with white, off-white, or pastels is the worst thing you can do. The extreme contrast between the light walls and dark furniture worsens your problem: The dark wood will seem even darker.

Large furniture or bulky pieces can also stand out awkwardly on a pale background. If your dining room looks too full, or your grandmother's suite too big for the room, add color to the walls to melt the furniture into its background and reduce the contrast between walls and wood. And as a bonus your dining room will come alive, because a colorful wall can bring out colors in the wood grain of your furniture.

Try this in the kitchen too. Too many cabinets? Too dark? Woodwork overwhelming? Use color. We tend to love wood because it has color, variation, and personality. No two pieces of wood are alike. Wood is alive. But when you surround wood with an un-color, it dies; it just looks brown. Every wood species is a composition of wonderful colors—reds, oranges, yellows, greens, even purples—and wood needs color as a backdrop to bring out these natural colors. Even fake-wood cabinets look better against color. After all, their surface is a true "picture" of a wood grain, so the same principle applies.

Visit a high-end furniture store, one that sells antiques, handcrafted wood pieces, and current imports. You will rarely see these merchants display their treasures against white or pastel walls. They sell wood against color to play up the grain.

Challenge: **My furniture is too big for my house; color will worsen the situation.**

Solution: *Wrong! The less contrast between the walls and the dark furniture, the smaller your furniture will appear and the larger your room will feel! Pick up a piece of colored poster board from a paper store—even solid-color wrapping paper will do. Hold a sizable piece of color next to the furniture in question, and look at a similar size area of the furniture piece. You will see your colors dance! Try this at different times of day. Your furniture will look significantly better.*

It's hard to evaluate the relationship between the quantity of furniture and its given space, so let common sense be your guide. First let's look at some problems, then the solutions:

SMALL SPACES. In a modest New York apartment, for instance, wall-to-wall furniture is the norm. Space may be at a premium, but certain basic needs still must be met: storage, seating, sleeping, and so on. The result? Lots of furniture stuffed into an exceptionally small area.

DINING ROOMS AND KITCHENS. The predominance of woods, which gobble up light, produces a heavy look.

The solution is actually inspired by a theatrical technique: disappearance through matching the foreground with the background. Translated to your home, this means lessening the contrast between the background or wall color and the furniture in

ABOVE LEFT: No, you don't need white walls to lessen the effect of a large wood furniture piece. ABOVE RIGHT: Notice how the colorful walls blend this armoire into the room. The visual weight of the colorful walls also balances the heft of the large furniture piece.

question. This accomplishes two effects. First, the largeness or darkness of the object is minimized as the furniture piece blends into the background. Second, the richer the color surrounding the wood pieces, the more obvious and exciting the wood grain.

I know what you're thinking: "Won't this solution create an overly darkened room with a reduction of visual space?" Not necessarily. Although the room is darker, the bulk has been tamed—a worthwhile compromise. Design is a series of such tradeoffs. A beautiful room is achieved in many cases by taking the edge off uncomfortable conditions. The battle between light walls and dark, oversize furniture seems never-ending. Bringing some color to the situation settles the argument and often creates a room so wonderful that questions of size become unimportant.

The photos opposite demonstrate how much wood changes in the presence of color. The burled veneer is pretty but looks flat against the off-white wall. The darker parts of the grain seem even darker, and the lighter areas lack warmth. The piece even looks bulky—larger than you would want for the corner arrangement.

In the second picture the colors in the grain are more obvious. The golds and reds are more dominant. The wood is exciting. The grains dance. Paint the wall, and the armoire looks more in scale with its placement. It "belongs" to the wall rather than standing out against it.

P.S.: Isn't it interesting how the floral picture also changes? In the off-white room the picture seems small because the white wall absorbs the white of the mat. Your eye is drawn only to the coral flower head.

In the green room the picture seems larger by virtue of the contrast between the white mat and the wall color. The green of the wall enhances the greens in the picture, so you see the whole rather than a part.

ABOVE LEFT: Bold yellow subdues an oversize armoire. ABOVE RIGHT: A rosy color blends this bed into the wall.

In the lovely dining room, *above left,* another armoire settles into its space, this time thanks to a background of brilliant yellow, which enhances the yellows in the wood grain. Any sunny color would have brought the sun colors forward from the grain. Look at your woods and try to isolate the dominant color. If the tone is warm, as in pine and oak, autumn colors will enhance the lighter parts of the grain and brighten the piece. Cool colors will enrich the darker areas of the grain for a beautiful effect.

Color can diminish bulky, oversize, and overly dominant objects, including bedding. One of the challenges of decorating bedrooms is dealing with a queen- or king-size mattress in a medium-size room. The bed takes over the room, and nothing can compete. The solution is to use color to link the bedding area and the wall. In the bedroom, *above right,* the warm color in the bedding was applied to the walls for balance. Ah, instant relief! The balance creates calm.

Color lightens up a roomful of wood furniture. The wall color also keeps a grand window treatment from overpowering the space.

When you walk into a room, is your window treatment the first thing you notice? Uh-oh. How did that happen? Maybe you were just moving a little too fast. Too often window treatments are the first items purchased after moving into a new home. The practical need for light control and privacy often drives homeowners to make a premature decision on pattern, color, and construction. And if you get carried away, the window treatment can become overwhelming and appear out of balance with the rest of the room.

Well, next time remember that a window treatment is not anywhere close to the top of the list of priorities in planning a well-designed room; it's much closer to the bottom. For now, one way to tame a window treatment that is grandstanding is to color it out by painting the walls either the dominant color or the background color of the fabric.

Walls clad in wood paneling or brick will absorb furniture just as the colorful painted walls do in the previous examples. Look at the room below and try to imagine how this weighty headboard (made from an old door) and the heavy tapestry bedcover would look against a pastel or off-white wall instead of this brick one. The contrast would be too much; the furnishings would appear too heavy. Here, the woods, tapestry, and brick walls make a wonderful combination, even in this very small bedroom in a loft apartment. The dark of the brick absorbs the dark of the bed set. (Had the walls not been brick, rolling on a rich wall color would have served a similar purpose.) The result is a richly textured environment. Size is irrelevant in a beautiful and cozy room.

In the East Coast kitchen on the next page, were the cabinets colored into the walls or the walls colored to absorb the cabinets? Which came first? Well, let's say this

Brick walls balance the rugged wood furniture pieces and the weighty tapestry-patterned bed cover.

ABOVE LEFT: Wood cabinets blend into matching walls. ABOVE RIGHT: In contrast, light walls show off the beauty of rugged shutters and architecture.

was your kitchen and the house came with teal Shaker-style cabinets and an off-white wall. If the high-ceiling walls were kept an "un-color," they would tower over the cabinets, and the cabinets would look much larger because of the color contrast. Thanks to the colored walls, your eye now goes to the view, the French door, the food, and the flowers because the cabinets have been absorbed into the wall. This is a rich color and yet the boundaries of the room disappear. The exterior, the view, and the light—these are the main events.

In defense of white: We've been talking about the negative aspects of wood and white, but there are positive features about this combination as well. Sometimes you want your woods to stand out and take a bow. In the Southwest, walls are commonly white or cream because smooth stucco is the indigenous interior wall material. Historically walls were white or the red of the earth and wood was scarce. The wood here is a textural decorative treatment. Grain is less important. The rounded corners and molded shapes of the Southwest interior need the bolder contrast between wood and white. But spatial relationships don't change; lighter-color upholstery is used to offset the bulk and form a link to the light walls.

myth#6 "My home has an open floor plan, so I have to use the same color scheme throughout the house."

Reality: Let the furniture and accessories in each area make individual schemes. Think of the walls and floors in an open-concept plan as a backdrop to the activity that occurs within each room. One color or degrees of the same color create continuity from room to room. *If you would like the sense of color change or a new scheme as you move from dining area to living area to foyer, for example, work your colors into your upholstery selections and accessories, using the background wall color as the connector.* This is easy with neutral backgrounds such as camel, sand, sage green, dusty gray-blue, medium apricot, haze-gold. These colors will accommodate both warm and cool combinations.

There is another option, however, if you wish to shift the background color from room to room. As you move from space to space, you can work within the same color family, using versions from light to dark, intensifying or lightening the color as you move through the floor plan. You can even use adjacent shades of those same neutrals. To change color from space to space, tucking the change line into inside and outside corners, is not that easy. Rooms and walls are rarely seen straight on. Most surfaces are viewed at an angle. That means you see two walls at the same time, meeting in an outside or inside corner. When the color change or shift is obvious, the "split" or "seam" in the "picture" can be distracting. A blended, continuous vista will

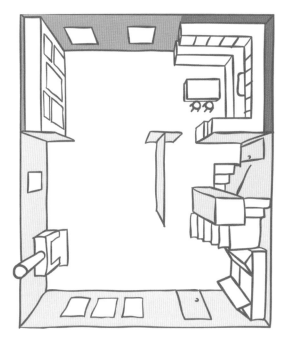

Subtle variations of the same wall colors create a harmonious, blended vista in an open-plan home.

probably feel more comfortable to you, keeping your attention on what is in the room rather than its background.

Of course, the absolute answer is to paint all the spaces which converge in one color, which is why it's best to vary your scheme with colorful furnishings and accessories versus changing wall colors. The architect intended the open plan to read as one interconnected and flowing area, which is why color continuity is important. After all, didn't you choose the home's plan for its continuity, flow, and open movement? If you start breaking up the space with a variety of colorfully painted or papered walls, you will defeat the purpose of the design and create an architectural monster in the process. It will never feel right to you. Your instincts will tell you that your home has lost its integrity.

Challenge: **My home has an open-concept floor plan. You can see from one room to**

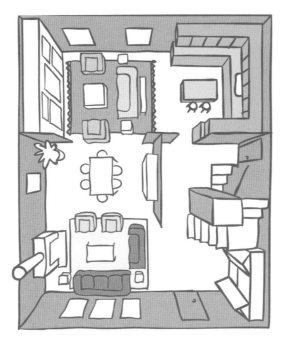

The wall color remains the same for continuity, but the colors of furnishings shift from area to area to define the spaces.

to another. I want to use some color but don't know where to stop and start it.

Solution: *Choose one color you love—a natural color (such as a tan or a green) that accommodates all other colors—and use the same background color in all connecting areas. Shift your color schemes from room to room by changing the colors of furnishings and accessories in each area. The background color will provide the continuity.*

myth#7 "I don't know where to start, so it's best to do nothing."

Reality: Start at the beginning of this book, and don't paint until you've finished!

I think I have heard it all when an audience member approaches me after a live lecture on color and asks what color she should paint her walls. The litany goes like this: I ask, "What color is your floor?" She responds, "Off-white." I ask, "What color is your sofa?" She responds, "Off-white." "What color is your furniture?" "Pale pine."

"Do you have anything in your room that must be coordinated into your scheme? Is there something I am missing?" "No, everything is off-white so it goes with everything!" I finally ask, "Why are you having so much trouble choosing a color when you could put anything on your walls?" And she says, "I'm afraid I won't like it." But I sympathize. It's like having a closet full of beige clothes. Elegant color. Dress it up or down. Always tasteful. After five years of beige you go shopping for a suit. You're with a friend. You are in the dressing room and the store attendant brings you a bright coral suit, to which you respond, "I couldn't wear that!" It's only natural if you haven't experienced color in five years. You begrudgingly try it on, rebelling all

ABOVE LEFT: Start small with a soft new wall color as in this sitting spot. ABOVE RIGHT: Or, how about adding a dash of fresh color to a bland entryway by rolling on a coat of soft blue paint and accenting the scheme with wide blue picture matting and a touch of wallpaper?

the way. The attendant and your friend are amazed. "You look ten years younger and ten pounds thinner!" they exclaim. You buy the suit. Who wouldn't! You and coral were preapproved. Now you wear the color with confidence.

Think about this story when you are standing in front of those 3,500 colors in the paint department. Think about it again after you've summoned your courage to choose a wonderful color and your friends have exclaimed, "Look at your gorgeous new room! Did you buy new furniture? It looks fabulous! You're really good at this. Would you help me with my room?" Just smile.

Challenge: Everything I have is neutral. I'm ready for more color in my home, but I have no idea what to choose.

Solution: *Pick your favorite color. Look at your closet, your car, your favorite coffee mug. Everyone has favorites, and often couples have the same preferences. Forget about trend colors. Take a look outside, study a patch of zinnias, and you will see that every color is timeless and therefore always in style.*

myth#8 "My room faces west. Won't warm colors make the room feel hot?"

Reality: In general, this myth goes into the basket of "old wives' decorating tales—circa 1940s." There are so many influences on a room's color that to base your color choice on just one environmental element makes no sense.

Color can be affected by any one or a combination of the following factors, including landscaping outside the window and sunlight filtering through the color of the trees. Through a willow, the sun will cast a lime green. Through a dark fir tree, a blue-green is cast. If the light is bouncing off a neighbor's brick wall or colorful siding, it may shift your interior wall color. The sun will pick up the edges of a

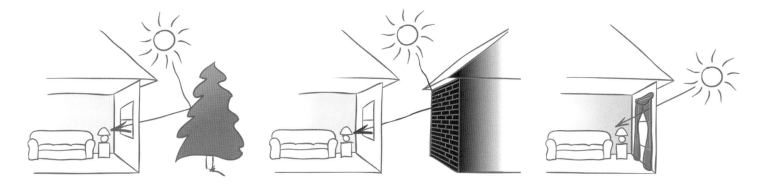

Reflecting off a green tree, bouncing off a brick wall, or shining straight inside, sunlight does affect the look of your interior's colors. Because those effects continually change as the sun moves during the day, my advice is to choose the color you want and let nature take its course.

colorful drapery and cast a tint. If you have colored sheers or horizontal or vertical blinds, their colors will affect your wall color too. Even if your walls are un-colored, nature is playing games with every surface every day. From spring to winter, rain to sunshine, your colors change as the light changes from blue in the winter to gold in the summer season. Too much to take into consideration? For most, yes. So my advice is this: Choose any color you want and let nature add its own touch. If you want burnt orange in a room that faces the sunset, do it! In the winter you'll feel cozy. (Besides, air-conditioning hadn't been invented when that old rule was made!)

Challenge: **Do I have to use cool colors in a south-facing room and warm colors in north-facing rooms? That seems so boring.**

Solution: *The answer is no. Many of these rules were made at a time when people lived in their homes much differently and their floor plans were limited. They didn't have the wide variety of window treatments that we have today to control light. Forget the old dictates and choose color according to your instinct rather than a rule that no longer applies. It's true that to some people cool colors, such as blue and green, may seem depressing in a north-facing room, because such rooms do not receive direct sunlight.*

However, to others, the effect may be simply restful. Similarly, red in a south-facing room may cause one person to turn on the air-conditioning while another may find that atmosphere purely romantic.

The picture below is one of my favorite scenes. The filtered light and pale blush wall color feel ethereal. But let's analyze the light: A springtime sun, shining through early green in the tree leaves outside the window, then filtering through off-white wood blinds, and passing through and around a semitransparent soft green swag, finally passes beyond the enclosure of the bay window alcove and lands on the wall color.

Now, do you think the lighting effects in the room on the previous page were planned? Absolutely not. Even the finest designers cannot analyze such numerous and often capricious lighting variables and predict the outcome. So don't get tangled

Who can predict all the lovely effects of sunlight filtering into a room? Relax, pick the colors you love, and then enjoy nature's surprises.

up in it. Simply choose your color, control what you can, and enjoy the surprises that nature throws at your room. Obviously, painting a wall yellow and covering a large window with red sheers would produce predictable results: Light through red sheers sends orange onto a yellow wall, turning it pale orange. But this is an extreme and obvious example. Just beware of full-coverage window treatments, such as sheers, in strong colors. The result under certain conditions can be similar to placing tinted bulbs in all of your light fixtures.

myth#9 "My real estate agent says white rooms sell houses!"

Reality: I say that white will not sell a house as well as a beautifully decorated room with wonderful color will!

Whitewashing your house to sell it is a low-risk proposition for an agent—and giving agents the respect they're due, one must realize that their job is to sell your home as quickly and painlessly as possible. But I will argue that a beautiful home, a home full of colorful personality, a home that feels good—like a home and not just a house—will be the most memorable, intriguing, and valuable to a prospective buyer. A home that conveys such good feelings says you that respect the architecture, that you've lovingly cared for the house, and that it has good "karma." This is an unbeatable combination sure to bring the best price and a good buyer.

Challenge: I'm selling my house and I need to freshen the walls. My agent says to paint it all white.

Solution: *Well, what I say is that a well-decorated home sells better than any specific color palette. What the agents are really looking for is a clean, airy, and uncluttered home. Rather than whiting out your rooms, pare down your accessories to the bare minimum.*

Would the colors in this elegant and inviting bedroom be an impediment to selling this house? Of course not.

Keep your home tidy, pull back the curtains, raise the blinds, and wash the windows!

P.S.: By the way, it is said that yellow houses sell faster than any other color!

Would you buy the house shown above? Is this room a negative? Even if the furnishings do not suit your personal style, would you walk away from this home simply because of the color of the bedroom? Most likely not. Would you care about the room's dimensions? Not as long as your own furniture would fit. Is the room memorable? *Absolutely.*

Do you have to have white? Doesn't "delightful" sell a home too? With cozy, dark walls balanced by whites and warmed by yellow fabrics and shining brass, this memorable dining room touches the imagination with dreams of languid brunches and happy occasions.

I find the dining room pictured above absolutely delightful. But take away the chairs and picture yourself painting these walls on a Saturday morning. Within 10 minutes, many of you would be running back to the paint department for a remix. Dark and scary? Coming out of the can and within a few hours of painting, maybe. Ah, but wait! Brighten the trim with white, place all of your furniture, add a glittering brass chandelier, and upholster a chair or four in brilliant yellow—or bright fuchsia or pumpkin!—and WOW! *Stick to your guns.*

color: the miseries of choice

Now that we've made "mulch" of your fears and excuses, let's pick a color.

A DESIGNER'S COLOR DECK FROM A SINGLE PAINT MANUFACTURER CONTAINS UP TO 6,000 COLORS! A PAINT DISPLAY IN A HOME IMPROVEMENT CENTER CAN CARRY AS MANY AS 2,500 COLORS PER BRAND. WHY? The manufacturers hope that out of the thousands of hues presented, at least one simple color will stir your soul.

But why so many confusing shades of the same colors, some only a nano-fraction different from their neighbor? *Good question.* It all has to do with the fact that no two people see a given color in exactly the same way. And any given color will not look the same in any two houses. Color is an abstraction. Think of it as tinted light. You can't contain light in a box. If you close up the box, there is no light inside. Open the box to let the light in, and it spills out at the same time. (That's one of those philosophical mysteries of life!) Light is produced by natural and artificial sources, and sometimes the combination of both. Your perception of a color is affected by surrounding colors, artificial lighting, natural light through windows, and your personal and psychological preference. I could show you a blush color. You may call it pink, and someone else might label it as peach. The root of pink is red, and the root of peach is orange.

This one is easy: Put blue next to yellow, and the blue will appear to be a touch green. Put the same blue next to red and you'll interpret the blue as being a little purple. The colors aren't changing; your brain is interpreting the colors differently. Look at the opposite page; what color is the stripe in the middle? Is it plain beige or off-white, or is it tinged with some other hue?

What color do you think this is?

Now look at the middle stripe on the opposite page. What color is it? Each stripe is pale pink, but note how the same color looks slightly different when it is surrounded by a pale blue and a pale magenta here versus when it was framed in white on the preceding page. To many, the color might appear to be "builder beige." *If your answer was pale pink,* you might have a particularly heightened sense of color or most likely a psychological preference for pink (maybe even red), so you saw your natural preference right away. You will always be drawn to that color range. Who knows where the preference comes from. Infantile imprinting? Maybe.

The point is that everyone has favorites that feel just right. Ask a preschooler what his or her favorite color is and you'll get an immediate answer. **What has happened to that childhood love of color, that spontaneity?** It's tough to draw on that early enthusiasm when you're standing in front of that intimidating color display in the paint department.

As we grow older we tend to surround ourselves with less and less color. Neutrals are sophisticated. Subtle. **Elegantly understated. Safe.**

Our adult color experience is often influenced by wardrobe preferences. A woman who consistently wears neutrals will feel comfortable in a room decorated in understated neutrals. A man who wears color well will respond positively to a more colorful decorating scheme.

In this chapter, we'll talk about how you can get going on the personal color scheme you've wanted—how to identify your "inspiration points" and build on those to create a palette that's just right for you.

start with what you have. AND WHAT YOU HAVE IS INSPIRATION. Don't say

you have nothing. It's all around you—in your furniture, a fabric, a picture, a chair, a tablecloth, even a tea towel or a favorite candy dish. Most color selection, even at the hands of a designer, begins with a piece of "inspiration"—something in your room that *you* chose. And you chose it because you liked it—maybe even loved it. Your color sense was working then, but of course, in all fairness, you weren't declaring your taste to the whole world on four walls, right? "After all, it's only a candy dish," you say. Well, have confidence in those choices. Build on each one.

Color schemes aren't invented out of thin air. They are inspired. You are surrounded by inspirational items that you purchased most assuredly because you liked the shape, usefulness, pattern, and COLOR.

What are your favorite things? Get color inspiration from the objects around your house.

Pick an item you love and study it for a moment. Write down the colors you see and like. Look at the mix and proportion—how much of one or another is in the design. There is your palette—in fact you can build a coordinated color scheme for a whole house around one such item.

Professional artists compose colors for wallpaper designs that you can use as a guide in creating your own palette.

If you really are starting with a blank slate and don't really care for anything you have—or if maybe you just need a new idea—wallpaper books may be your best friend. Professional graphic and fine-art designers spend their careers developing color, balance, and scale in hundreds of interpretations. They compose with color. Like a symphony or opera, a color scheme has a lead, a melody—that is, a hierarchy of colors spread around the pattern in certain proportions. There is a background color (maybe your walls?), a dominant color in the motif (your sofa?), secondary and tertiary colors (for accents?) in every pattern.

the I'd-rather-die-than-not-match club. DON'T JOIN THIS ONE!

Color is abstract. Until it is mixed or rendered in paint or any other medium, it is imaginary. And like any concept that is held only in your mind's eye, color is imprecise. You may envision the perfect yellow or blue, but by the time you find the paint chip, the computerized match, and the wallpaper with exactly the background you are looking for, you have been influenced by variables that compromise your original idea. Imagine the perfect color and then go looking for it among the thousands of paint chips in the display: You'll be frustrated. First there's the commercial lighting in the store, which is different from the lighting in your home. Then there's the effect of the color group display adjacent to it in the chip rack, which shifts the hue: For instance, when yellow is displayed next to green, it looks more yellow-green. The lighting at home changes with the seasons, the time of day, and the weather. Window treatments, tinted lampshades, and a strong-colored floor will shift the color as well. So, how can you choose a color with confidence?

Color is not finite. Choosing color is an imperfect science. It is no more precise than predicting the shifting shades of your garden from year to year.

To shop with a fabric swatch in hand, determined to find a "dead match," is a never-ending exercise that will drive you to distraction. Color reads differently from one material to another. You may place a fabric sample under a color-matching machine in the paint department, but the results will not be perfect once you apply the paint to the wall. Your fabric is made up of various natural and synthetic fibers woven at right angles to each other. Fibers running in different directions pick up the light differently. The fabric most likely is used on a horizontal or shaped object, such as your sofa, or it

might be sewn into a window treatment that manipulates light into shadows and folds, again rendering the color differently. The painted surface of your walls, although supposedly the "exact" color match of the fabric, will look different due to the walls' smooth texture and vertical position. In addition, the color will look slightly different on each wall, because the light, whether coming through a window or shining from a lamp, will strike each wall surface with varying degrees of intensity. **Stop matching! Coordinate. Group.** Put four blues together and they look wonderful: three yellows, five reds, and so on. *When you decorate with several shades of the same color, it gives you tremendous freedom to "grow" the room:* Add and subtract for as long as you live there without the pressure of always finding the elusive "perfect match."

finding your colors.

DESIGNERS EXTRACT THEIR COLORS from an existing item, a fabric swatch, a work of art, a scenic view, a greeting card, a tie, even a centerpiece. Designers are always searching for interesting combinations, watching how light plays on certain groupings. Sure, designers get lots of practice. But more helpful than practice is the art of seeing color as a liquid form. Add water to a drop of paint, push it around on watercolor paper, and watch the original color droplet take on a range of personalities. This variable nature of color is what designers learn to appreciate and work with to create a beautiful but relaxing environment.

When you approach a color scheme with a limited number of colors, there is tremendous pressure to confine your choices to matches, for fear that a certain non-matching item will look out of place. **The more colors or variations of colors in a room, the more freedom you have to add or subtract comfortably.** In your living room, for instance, look at your sofa fabric, a companion chair, draperies, even a picture or a decorative lamp base. Anything qualifies. **If you like the way the colors go together,** their proportions, the intricate subtleties, let that object be your inspiration. **You've just discovered the basis for your color scheme.** Let's build on it.

But before we go further, let's examine how the rooms that make up a house connect to each other. Why look at the whole house when you only want to choose one wall color for one room? Because rooms are not islands. They share borders with each other. As you walk from one room to another, did you know that you mentally carry the color scheme of one room into another for three seconds. It doesn't seem as if three seconds would matter, does it? But it makes the difference between a house that flows comfortably and one that feels disjointed, like a collection of rooms from different houses. **Color is the grand connector.**

Depending on the architectural style of your home, individual rooms are connected either through closed doors or open archways. They may be separated by hallways, or they may flow from one to another in an open-concept floor plan. Think of all the common area rooms as being related. Even if the furnishings in those "connected" rooms have different color schemes, there is a way to choose colors to pull the entire floor plan together. It's actually quite simple. It is a diagrammatic system of charting what you already have in your home, room by room, and finding the common denominators. If you're starting from scratch with a brand-new home or apartment and have many choices to make, this will become your master plan from which to "grow" each room in the future.

This is how it works: **First you need to identify that special piece of inspiration.** Most often it's a piece of fabric from a sofa, chair, or drapery treatment in the living room or an adjacent room, but this doesn't have to be the case. Schemes can be created from a painted scene on a lamp base, a needlepoint pillow, a wallpaper border, or a favorite area rug.

Whatever your piece of inspiration, your next step is to identify the three most dominant colors in it. The simple way to do this is to pick the three most obvious colors in terms of vividness or quantity. But you might be influenced by the complexities of the pattern. So I often ask a class of decor students to look at these chosen bits of inspiration from about 10 feet away and with their vision blurred—either by removing glasses or crossing the eyes—to obscure the pattern.

Here's the reason for this somewhat silly procedure: Too often color confusion arises from looking at fabrics and color swatches in an unrealistic situation. Your perception of a pattern can change dramatically if you change the distance from which you see it. Look at a person's face at too close a range, and all you see is a nose, a mouth, and two ears. You don't have a sense of what the person really looks like. You lose the symmetry and balance. Proportion and scale are exaggerated. The effect your sofa fabric has on your room is from a distance and not up close. When you are sitting or napping on your sofa, of course you see it up close—but not in relation to the room. You experience the overall impact that your sofa fabric has on the room when you enter, pass through, or walk around in the living room. Like seeing a face from a distance, you see all the pattern and color and its scale according to its environment. To appreciate the artistry and colors so beautifully balanced in your sofa, you should observe from a natural and contextual distance—about 10 to 12 feet away. As for the blurry vision: This helps you ignore the lines and composition of the pattern, which may otherwise confuse your eye and cause you to incorrectly rank one color as more important than another.

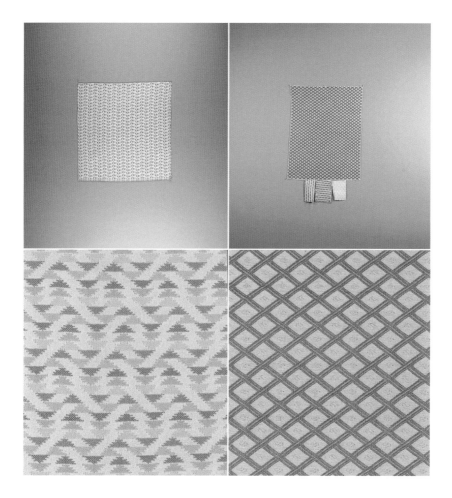

Here you see two fabrics at two distances. We photographed these with the camera lens at a position that shows the fabrics as your eye might see them. On the bottom, you see the fabric up close, about 14 inches away from your eyes—your distance when choosing the fabric or enjoying the sofa from the vantage point of an afternoon snooze. The top two pictures show the sofa fabric in the context of the room as you enter—at a distance of 10 feet. Now which colors are dominant? The answer may be the same from 10 feet as it is at 14 inches, but in some cases you'll find a dramatic difference. When choosing a fabric, you need to be aware of such variations in perception. Your affinity for a certain color is still what counts. No matter how you look at a fabric, if there is one particular color in that pattern that you adore, it's likely you'll see it as being in either first or second place.

Once you have determined the three dominant colors, take your sample to the paint department of a home improvement center to find the paint chips that come closest to those three colors. Usually the colors on the chips are graded from light to dark. Find the chips that contain colors that come as close as possible to your three fabric colors. DO NOT TRY TO DEAD-MATCH. The chances are slim that you will be able to. And remember that matching is not the answer. Related color is close enough.

Practice now by pretending that this is your sofa. Scrunch your eyes and choose the three most dominant colors in this fabric.

On the chip you will find three or more versions of the same color or color family that will coordinate with your color. Add a fourth color, as we did in the chips shown above, and you create even more color options: With 3 colors per chip times 3 or 4 dominant colors, you'll have 9 to 12 colors for your palette. If you are working with a paint line that shows 5 colors per chip, you will have 15 to 20 color possibilities for your palette. Options, options, options!

Think about what has just happened: You and a professional graphic designer, the author of that fabric or wallpaper from which you isolated your colors, someone you've never met, have found your color scheme. This is no-fear decorating! Now let's put those colors to work.

use my "color charting system." THE NEXT STEP IS TO MAKE A CHART

that looks like the one on the opposite page, listing your rooms down the side. Start with the front door and work up from the ground floor through the bedrooms and bathrooms and then down to the lower-level rec-room/basement areas. Don't forget to count hallways. Across the top of your chart, write the letters A through E from left to right. These boxes represent color uses in order of priority. A is for the floor and B for walls: These are the most dominant and the largest areas of color. A and B are interchangeable, depending on the architecture or the floor plan. C refers to the third largest area of color in the room or to the third most impactful color object. This could be a large piece of upholstered furniture, a window treatment, or the ceiling. D and E are accent colors in descending order: D is the fourth largest area of color, such as an accent chair or a small rug; and E is the fifth, such as pillows, a footstool, collectibles.

YOUR HOME	A FLOOR	B WALLS	C 3RD LARGEST	D ACCENT 1	E ACCENT 2
LIVING ROOM	DARK GREEN	MEDIUM YELLOW	DARK TEAL	LIGHT PEACH	DARK YELLOW
DINING ROOM					
HALLWAY					
POWDER ROOM					
KITCHEN					
FAMILY ROOM					
STAIRWAY					
HALLWAY					
MASTER BEDROOM					
MASTER BATH					
BEDROOM 2					
BEDROOM 3					
BEDROOM 4					
ETC.					

Here's the process of filling in your chart: First lay out your color chips. If your chips have three versions of each of your "inspirational" colors, you most likely have three versions of each, from light to dark. If you have pulled out four dominant colors from your swatch, as I did, you now have 12 professionally chosen colors to work with.

How do you make a color scheme for a whole house from 12 colors without every room looking identical? What you will see is a subtle connection between areas. This is the understated coordination that you recognize as a well-decorated home. It's called "flow." Flow refers not only to traffic patterns, but to the visual relationships between rooms. Flow can be accomplished through color connectivity. But the real secret to this system, and the reason the rooms are not boringly similar, is that the colors change priority or dominance as they move from one room to another. The dominant color on the wall of the living room, for instance, might be a medium version of a sage green, but it will appear in the kitchen as a pale sage on an accent tile on the backsplash. The main color on the walls of the dining room may be a rich terra-cotta, which will emerge in its palest version as a pale peach in the hall. As colors change priority on the chart, they change their significance in each room. Our paint chips opposite show variations of the fabric's dominant colors—blue, peachy-rose, yellow, and green. Based on those, I filled in the first line of the chart, anchoring the living room with a dark green carpet (A), painting the walls a medium yellow (B), and planning dark teal (C) for a large accessory and light peach (D) for a small one. And imagine how beautiful a dark yellow footstool (E) would look in that context!

YOUR HOME	A FLOOR	B WALLS	C 3RD LARGEST	D ACCENT 1	E ACCENT 2
	DARK GREEN	MEDIUM YELLOW	DARK TEAL	LIGHT PEACH	DARK YELLOW
LIVING ROOM					
DINING ROOM					
HALLWAY					
POWDER ROOM					
KITCHEN					
FAMILY ROOM					
STAIRWAY					
HALLWAY					
MASTER BEDROOM					
MASTER BATH					
BEDROOM 2					
BEDROOM 3					
BEDROOM 4					
ETC.					

These additional companion fabrics reinforce the color scheme. I've mixed tone-on-tone solids with multicolor patterns that repeat the colors in the main fabric swatch. As you mix your own patterned fabrics, look for companion prints that vary in scale from the dominant print. Avoid using two patterns of the same scale.

Now let's add a new pattern. This time we chose a new fabric for place mats and a table runner—a pattern that has many of our basic colors as well as new shades of pale blue. Back to the paint department we go to identify the associated blue paint chips. Now we have three more colors with which to play. By adding these, we can create a richer palette and avoid a scheme that looks too "matchy-matchy."

You can use this color charting system in two ways: First, you can plan a new color scheme for your home. Second, you can fill in the chart with colors that you already have in each room. Using the chart as a color inventory, you may find that the color answer you were searching for already exists in another room. And you will begin to see what's working (and what isn't) in your rooms. You may notice colors, surfaces, furnishings, or accessories that have no connection to anything else in the vicinity. There may not be anything wrong with that—or you may see that such a lack of color connections is the root of some dissatisfaction that you've felt with a particular room. This color inventory process can be revealing. Your first reaction might be, "Wow, I not only solved my problem in one room but can see exciting opportunities in several others!" You can't change everything at once, but with this chart, you can see where you are —and begin building a road map to your design goal.

The reds in this room's patterned fabrics inspired the warm wall color. Starting with the same fabrics, how might you chart your own scheme?

a bit of black.

ACTUALLY, BLACK ISN'T THE POINT. The theory is that a bit of dark in a room anchors the color scheme.

Like white trim, a portion of dark, as an edge or an object, clarifies color. Imagine for a moment a photograph that is unframed and held up against a wall—not a very interesting image, is it? Now envision that same photograph framed in black—the picture's image has newfound crispness and clarity. Like that black mat around a photograph, black in a room sharpens and finishes color that floats off the edge. It creates depth, emphasizing shadow and shape. Look at these pictures and notice where your eye is drawn. Try to envision the room opposite and those on the following pages without their touches of black.

Adding black/dark isn't expensive. Use a single cushion on a sofa or side chair, a black lampshade, a black art object, a black mat on an appropriate picture, a black background in an area rug. Nearly every color scheme can benefit from black.

Take one basic living room—elegant, timeless, filled with neutrals. OK so far. Beige sofas and chairs atop a beige or sisal rug like this make a great starting point for a classic scheme. The white walls and trim add crispness to such neutrals. But something would be missing....

Could it be a touch of *black*? Of course. The black chest, used as a coffee table, adds instant drama and punch to the beige seating pieces—an effect enhanced by dark pillows and touches of black metals. A warm array of jacketed books bearing touches of black and other hues completes the picture. Now take a look at two more examples

Touches of black and dark brown add a sophisticated edge to this living room. Note how the contrast between dark and light intrigues your eye!

of the power of black. The yellow and black combination in the tiny mud room below is clean, cheerful, and very stylish. It's a makeover. *Ordinary cabinetry gains fresh style with new black iron knobs, a black countertop, and black picture frames.* Replacing the black with white would have been acceptable, even pretty. But it probably would have screamed for pattern or more accessories. A touch of black takes ordinary to sophisticated. Now, look at one of my favorite kitchens, *opposite*. Imagine it without the black countertops, the dark detail at the crown, and the black metal in the light fixture. The black is what makes you notice the carved detailing in the legs of the island and in the door panels. Black carves depth into adjacent elements. Your eye sees a bit of black and looks for other black/dark. Dark in this case is shadow. Shadow signals depth and helps you see texture and dimension in the room.

ABOVE: Yellow paint can only go so far in adding oomph to a lineup of white cabinets; bits of black create the sophisticated edge.

OPPOSITE: Take away the touches of black, and this kitchen would go flat. Shadows created by black sculpt the space, adding dimension.

coloramerica

From sea to shining sea
America's changing landscape and light impact
how we decorate. Deep in our psyches,
we have an innate sense of
the indigenous colors
of earth and sky.

TO ME, COLOR IS THE ROMANCE OF OUR ENVIRONMENT. IT IS THE ESSENCE OF LIGHT-PLAY AND OF THE INTERCONNECTION OF ALL NATURAL THINGS. It is a mood—for a fleeting moment tangible, yet ever fading or brightening. Color is the reflection of our geography.

Where you live and how you live in your home, how you decorate, how you choose color in your wardrobe, how you see color—all of this is affected by a geographic color palette that's as old as primitive man. An obvious example is the Southwest. Artists who experience the brilliance of the light and color in Arizona or New Mexico will never paint in quite the same way again in any other part of the country. Some say the light and color in the Southwest is surreal. Is it a scientific phenomenon—a hazeless turquoise sky and the blood orange/red earth—a vibration of contrasting colors? Every time I come around the corner on Highway #17 from Oak Creek, I gasp at the canyon colors of Sedona as if seeing them for the first time. Startling. It is a stunning part of America—filled with spirituality many say. But I wonder, if you took away the color, hazed the skies, and turned red rock to gray granite, would I come away with the same yearnings to return? Doubtful. Color is working the mystical.

Why is it that so many vacationers are so taken with these indigenous schemes that they transport them into a newly renovated family room in Minneapolis, or a kitchen in Hartford, or a powder room in St. Louis? Pale coral, soft turquoise, and Anasazi-inspired wallpaper borders in Des Moines? Others fall in love with the gray-weathered colors of the Northeast fishing villages. In Oklahoma City, an East Coast summer vacation may inspire a dusty-weathered-cool-taupe color for a farmhouse once

Southwestern decorating schemes usually rely on naturals with a reddish cast—a range of colors inspired by the region's rocks and soils and intensified by dazzling light and a turquoise sky. Those same colors die when transplanted to a Northeast coastal area where sea mist "grays" the light.

painted bright yellow, in an environment of warm golden wheat fields. Oops? Is it improper to transport one region's indigenous colors to another? Out of context? Architecturally dishonest? All debatable. Sometimes it works. But much of the time it doesn't. It *feels* wrong. We travel to expand our knowledge and experience and, we hope, to integrate our new experiences into our lives and enrich our futures. If you are design-receptive, color, shape, and form are all elements that impress you—you can't help but consciously absorb them and take them with you. So why is it that some of these regional palettes don't transplant?

Why do the vivid coral and deep turquoise of the Southwest look different in Minneapolis? **The light is different.** Light bounces around to pick up color from one environmental feature and then tint another. The turquoise sky in Sedona makes the red rock redder. But on a high-cloud, gray-weather day, even with the sun peeking through, that red is far less vivid. The rock hasn't changed, but because the light has diminished, the bright contrast isn't there. Take an exact replica of those vivid colors to the cooler light of the northern Midwest, and the colors will die in the light that filters through maples and oaks and bounces off rich farm soils. What happens to the dusty, weathered East Coast colors when they are translated to a wheat field farmhouse? The golden aura of the field makes the sea-mist-affected grays look drab, plain, dingy, old. Just as the sun spills through a picture window and bounces the deep green of your carpet onto a white wall and tinting it a soft green. The same sun

In the Southwest, a brilliant turquoise sky can't help but inspire similar colors in decorative fabrics, tile, and paint. Navy blue? No, not here.

bounces off a wheat field and tints its environment ever so slightly golden. Our light source is a constant—the sun through our atmosphere. The variables exist within and on the land—think of it as the color of our topography.

The earliest inhabitants of the varied regions of America decorated their dwellings, clothing, tools, and accessories with colors derived from their environment. Dyes were made from flowers, seeds, roots, charcoal, chalk pigments. Decorative elements—precious stones, shells, glass—became valuable marks of status sold through intersecting trade routes.

Color is relative. Early native women took their inspiration from the vivid colors of their environment in the Southwest. Turquoise, the color of the sky, was preferred over the softer shades. Deep, rich saturated ochers and dark blues were preferred to lesser hues. In contrast to their boldly hued environment, pastels would have appeared weak. The reverse is true in the Northeast where the bleached colors of the sea and the shorelines are all a delicate balance of whitened pastels created by the bleaching effects of salt air. Early people there were influenced by their grasses, white birch, and bone. In that context, rich, saturated color would have appeared gaudy.

Although we could dig deeper into the history of regional color preferences, let's jump forward to our current color cultures, which are equally influenced by the natural environment.

Somehow, deep in our color psyche, as intimidated and confounded by personal color choices as we may be, we have an innate sense of indigenous color. Otherwise color choices would not be as typecast by region as they still are today. The Northeast is still gray-washed and salt-weathered—deliberately! People there choose to paint their houses in sea-blasted colors. An homage to history? Maybe. Or maybe they know that the alternative wouldn't work within their existing environmental colors which still today include pale sand and shell tints plus the teal blue and angry green of the deep ocean. Since the first settlements, southern Floridians have been coloring their homes in pale pinks, aquamarine, and soft lime. Again, this is in tune with nature's own color scheme—the ocean is pale aquamarine, and the earth is sand-white, aged corals are pink, and palm trees splatter dappled shades of yellow-green and lime.

When we speak of "naturals" in the context of interior decoration, **what comes to mind is a beige/tan palette.** That's unfortunate, because the root of all color—its source, its manipulation—is nature. In fact it would be very hard to separate man-made colors from those conceived in the wilds.

indigenous regional colors: the real naturals. TRUE CONFESSION:

I have always been a "naturals" person. "Horrors!" you say, shocked at my career-long encouragement to use color.

If you define naturals as shades of beige, you would be justified in your reaction. However, colors classified as naturals include the entire spectrum. There is a "natural" shade of every color you can think of. Without getting too tricky I would describe naturals as a slightly diminished version of the supersize crayon box.

It's not surprising that so many of us choose to decorate with natural colors. Naturals are easy to live with for one good reason: We are subconsciously influenced by our regional colors during every waking moment. We live in those colors in our clothing choices, decorate our homes with indigenous colors, drive cars dictated by local color preferences. We feel comfortable, safe, a part of the whole. Step outside that scheme and you get nervous.

So why don't we all just color our lives in our regional colors and call it a day? Because we have an innate sense of individuality. Because we want to make our mark, sign our space, make our home our personal domain—and so we should.

I've met thousands of color-troubled homeowners in my career, and I divide them into two categories: the naturals and everyone else! There are those who simply cannot live outside a natural palette—so they shouldn't. But let's stretch that palette beyond beige.

For starters, I decided to get to the root of indigenous American color by starting with America's soil. We contacted people from all over the United States and asked them to send a small bag of dirt from an unlandscaped area close to their home— virgin dirt! What a marvelous range of colors! I was hooked. I couldn't stop until I was able to investigate the natural influences of six major regions. The results have become my personal palette.

Dirt from across America comes in an amazing array of colors. Gold, taupe, coral, green, even purple-tinged earth can inspire a natural palette.

For evidence, look at how beautifully these paint color cards work with the dirts we gathered from coast to coast.

is your color cue just outside the window?

The cool colors of the Maine woods influenced this home's exterior and interior colors. Light filtering through the leafy trees tints the living room— an effect that's played up by green decorative accents.

"but I love beige."

OK, I give up—
but only if you can tell me you are passionate about the colors beige, tan, bone, camel, cream, vanilla, sand, khaki, grass, wheat....

IF YOU WANT TO DECORATE WITH VARIOUS SHADES OF BEIGE, I WON'T ARGUE WITH YOU—AS LONG AS YOU ARE CONSCIOUSLY CHOOSING SUCH NEUTRALS BECAUSE YOU LIKE THEIR COLORS and not because you are simply afraid to commit to a color. Blame the builders, paint manufacturers, and retailers for creating the "un-color" default: four basic shades of off-white: yellowy off-white, pinky off-white, blue-y off-white, and peachy off-white. *How did we get here?* Subdivision home builders in the '70s knew that homeowners would personalize their homes after moving in, so why paint a color? Colors cost more, and someone would have to decide what color went where—too much trouble if homeowners would only repaint anyway. But white would look too antiseptic—too much like primed drywall, not a good image for a builder who cares. Off-white was the simple answer. Warm. Cheap. Easy. Paint manufacturers and retailers respond to the sales figures and demand: "Off-white is flying off the shelves! We'd better make more of it. Let's pre-mix it, and for a little pizzazz, make a tint card that shows several versions of off-white." It has become a vicious circle of bland.

With off-white walls, ceiling, and upholstery you run the risk of creating a blank canvas that engenders irritation instead of calm. White needs some contrast and depth. But remember: Anything dark will look bigger and bolder by contrast. That's why leaving the ceiling beams natural was a good call. The contrast enlarges the smallish beams to "just-right" size. A room should provide some sense of enclosure. Here, because the floor is dark, those sitting in this room might have felt as if the "lid" were off the place had the beams been painted the ceiling color. Now the room, although light, airy, and open to the outside, offers reassuring structure. The natural fiber area rug adds important texture. A monochromatic color scheme, regardless of the color, focuses the eye on whatever isn't the color. And when your attention is acutely focused on one item that is significantly different, you pick up the detail—texture, ornament, shape, and form. Now add the cushions: all white or with pattern? All white would have been cold; a bit of lighthanded pattern on a consistently white background scatters that essential bit of contrast around the line of sight. White all around with brown on the floor and in the middle table would be a strong visual. Sprinkling much smaller touches of contrast around the room relaxes the environment.

Then a year after the homeowners move into this beige box, they are still paying for the much-needed window treatments and the upgraded carpet. Piece by piece, they're still replacing the old make-do furnishings with new. "Color for the walls? Not yet. We're not finished decorating! And besides, off-white goes with everything anyway."

Three years later, a letter arrives in my office. As at least a third of the letters do, this one poses color questions: "Dear Lynette, My living room is boring. My sofa is a beige floral. We chose a tan carpet because it goes with everything. The window treatment is a tan stripe to match the sofa. My walls are off-white, and the ceiling is a white-sprayed gritty plaster. What's wrong?" Bland beige blahs.

Face-to-face, when I've offered people the suggestion of color and been able to observe their reaction, I've seen that I might as well have suggested a couturier makeover ending with a walk down a Parisian runway: "Me? Do that? Live with color? In *my* living room?" Most people really do want color. They may be terrified by the thought of it, but they know that's what's missing in their rooms.

So that's not you. You love—really *love*—beige and off-white. You see them as mellow, light, elegantly neutral. You love the way a neutral scheme shows off the colorful collectibles and contemporary black-and-white photography you adore. You have a delicate sense of balance, texture, and form. Wonderful! (And you thought I'd say "Yeccch!") Remember what I said earlier: In the end, the only thing that matters is what *you* feel comfortable living with.

Here are some of my favorite beige looks, each overcoming a particular challenge. Remember that every version of beige is a true color, so it needs attention just like any other color. What beige needs is white, something dark, tiny bits of color, lots of texture, and understatement.

Love artwork? Emphasize it, gallery-style, with white walls and wide white picture mats like these.

An all-white foyer organizes this space. The lack of color draws your eye to all of the woods: architectural moldings, floor, stairs, and table. White neutralizes wood to basic brown. Wood needs color to exaggerate the color in the grains. But here the woods are deliberately stained to contrast with each other: Red, gold, dark chocolate, and orange. Try to envision this hall and stair area without the contrasting woods, art, or accessories. The ceiling breaks away oddly above the stairs. The window is shoved into the corner. An old utilitarian stair is turned into beauty by neutralizing the envelope with white and then focusing your eye on wood architectural elements—and especially the graphic art. Finely detailed artwork needs a minimalist background. The combination of white walls and wide white mats puts the focus on the art itself, regardless of how small or finely executed. In a setting this simple, even a simple pitcher of garden flowers gets its due.

Neutral schemes demand textures. Imagine these rooms without their touches of nubby wicker.

Naturals and whites are made for each other. Whites reinforce textures. Whites also love geometry. In this bedroom, the neutrals play up the stripes and plaids, the herringbone weave of the wicker table, and the checkered sisal rug. To warm up whites, vary the stripes—wide on the walls, combinations on upholstery and accessories. White in a bathroom says clean, crisp, soapy, but **white walls, shiny white tile, and hard white fixtures quickly become clinical.** The fix? Texture and humanizing accessories. Above right, a stack of wicker adds contrasting texture and warmth. Taupe walls reinforce the white while softening the environment. Tureen lids balance the hard white fixtures by carrying the same look to the upper wall.

In low-light areas, deepen your off-whites to medium tans and taupes. Remember, when there is no light, pastels and whites won't make light. They'll just appear dingy.

ABOVE LEFT: The mix of dark and light taupes creates drama. ABOVE RIGHT: Slipcovers with a touch of color can brighten neutrals during a long winter.

Now, as you see in the bedroom above left, you at least have a color! Contrasting a deeper neutral with white trim, upholstery, and accessories snaps brilliance into the scheme for a look that's both cozy and crisp. Now the light that does make it into the room is emphasized by contrast.

There are certain times of year when we crave a little more color in our decorating "diets." The living room here is a good example of how you can maintain the off-white base but seasonally splash it with zest. For instance, when the weather turns dreary and the light is icy blue after the holidays, a dash of rainbow here and there can hurry spring. Slipcovers do the trick. But notice how the background of all the patterns is white or off-white. The white palette remains dominant. And although the colors in the patterns are brilliant, they're overpowered by the neutrals.

9

great beginnings

So, you're ready
to take that first colorful step,
but the thought of committing to brilliant color
throws you into a panic?
OK, OK. Let's start with just
a touch of color.

HOW ABOUT WALLS OF BRILLIANT COLOR—Mediterranean blue-green, van Gogh's sunflower yellow, a city-sophisticated eggplant, or retro pumpkin? "Yikes, I'm not that ready!" you say, body flattened against your beloved pastel walls. OK, OK.

Let's start with just a touch of color. Call it an experiment. Just a quart of paint here, a cushion there, maybe spring for one newly upholstered chair or ottoman. It doesn't take much color to inject a lot of zest into a room, a hallway, or even a corner. This is a wonderful opportunity for you to play. Think of your most favorite color. Your first reaction may be, "Oh, but it doesn't 'go' with what I have in the room." Who says? Maybe it's just that you haven't decorated with that color before, so it looks a little daring. You're afraid it doesn't "match?" That's a deep pit—don't go there. Or is the color only scary because it's new and your room has been the same for soooooo long? While it's true that, as soon as you introduce a new color area or a colorful object, your eye will dart to it the second you enter the room, give it time. Are you checking to see if it's still there? Just want to make sure you haven't done something dumb? Live with that color; integrate that color into your image of the room. Stop staring at it. It will come to you in its own due time and eventually be your best friend. Then add another.

Take a look at these spaces, which needed some color help. Try to imagine them without their punch of color. Pretty dull, eh? Along the way, think about how you can "feed" your own color-hungry rooms.

Against a backdrop of warm neutral walls and woods, purple upholstered dining chairs steal the scene. A few other small touches—a gathering of blooms here, a bowl of lemons there—and your colorful new scheme is complete! (Hint: Purple goes with everything. Try it!)

draw your inspiration from the colors around you.

Relax. Think about a colorful setting that draws you—a pond or a lake, for instance. Now bring those serene greens and blues up onto your porch or deck. Where would this lakeside porch be without its fresh, watery blue-green floor?

ABOVE AND OPPOSITE: Feeling braver now? Toss on a colorful patterned pillow or two so your eye can get used to color. By working with such changeable accents, you can experiment with colors without committing to something permanent. Ready to go a step further? Open the door, opposite, and let a bit of your newfound color bravery step inside. Here, bright new slipcovers add some shine and personality to a sunroom.

ABOVE AND OPPOSITE: Now look what a little color confidence can do! A collection of bold and beautiful Fiestaware, above left, gives color punch to a plain white kitchen. Once you let bits and pieces of changeable color invade your home—smack!—the next thing you know, you may be ready to commit to an intense wall color, such as the red in the bedroom, above right. Or, opposite, how about waking up an essentially neutral living room by splashing bright cushions, vases, and artwork around it?

experiment with small

Beige loves reds. In this setting, a monochromatic beige moves from blah to exciting with an oversize, two-color floral pattern made into pillows. If simple colorful pillows worry you, try experimenting with some posterboard. Cut pillow-size squares, and prop them on your furniture in pillow position. Use wrapping paper, scarves, or even a colorfully patterned blouse to mimic throw cushions for a few days. You'll feel much more comfortable shopping for pillow fabrics when you have predetermined your favorite looks.

touches of color
and pattern to find the right fit for your eye.

One of my favorite ways to play with a
little wall color without making a big
commitment is to spot color in and around
built-ins. The color brings the wood grain
to life. Warning: Painting one unframed
wall in a room always makes the room look
incomplete, unless you are attempting a
'60s retro concept. That's why I like to use
color on a wall like this, which is framed
and thus integrated into the room by the
wood of the built-ins.

get a big return
on a small color investment.

ABOVE AND OPPOSITE: Thinking about new upholstery or slipcovers? They offer a great way to inject color into a room. Not too loud, not a vague pastel—choose some color that you'll be prepared to live with for a while. Solution: Purple! It works with everything. Deep purple is actually a neutral. It's gorgeous with browns and golds. It gives an autumn color scheme a lift. Think of those gorgeous Japanese maples in the fall. This dark purple hides wear and tear while zapping neutrals with flair. It's understated and sophisticated. Do it!

color your life, one seat at a time.

Ready for some serious color? Upholster your sofa in brilliant yellow! You simply cannot be in a bad mood in this room. Place your hand over the sofa in this picture—what a difference! Especially for those of you who live in rental housing or apartments, a yellow sofa will add instant style to any room in any condition. And check those checks—yellow-and-white checkerboard side chairs. With courage like this, you needn't worry about the rest of the room. Just starting out and furniture-poor? One yellow sofa, a coffee table, a lamp, a pile of floor cushions, a large plant, and a sound-system, and you're set!

do something exciting
in your kitchen.

I love using aggressive color in the kitchen. Often, this is the room in your home with the least amount of visible wall space. A colorful wall can make a welcome accent to all of the other, more dominant surfaces. So do something exciting. Brilliant color makes food look wonderful. Even in a south- or west-facing kitchen with no direct sunlight early in the day, bright colors can create a happy morning. And if you entertain in the kitchen, as many of us do these days, you will have added a little drama to the evening. Beyond painted walls, kitchen color opportunities include back walls of exposed shelving, backsplashes, and bulkheads, painted or clad in laminate.

inter-space

Think your room is too small or too big? Maybe it just feels that way. Whether your space problem is about square footage or feelings, there's always a solution.

SPACE—NOW THERE'S AN ABSTRACTION. Try to describe a specific space without a room name, and you fumble through a vocabulary of vague emotional phrases crossed with numerical assumptions. A precious architectural commodity, space is the stock-in-trade of designers and architects, whose objective is to make it functional, livable, emotionally satisfying. Yes, an abstraction.

It's intriguing that space—a concept that is defined by numbers—has such enormous emotional influence on the way we live and how we respond to our environment. Various formulas and charts average out the natural scale—the reach and stride—of human beings. And through ergonomic and kinetic study, we know within a micro measure the average comfort level for every activity and have translated that into shapes and dimensions that accommodate our needs. And yet mere measurements do not tell the whole story.

From birth we are imprinted with space-related experiences: the crib, the playpen, the backyard, the park, the school playground. How do we see ourselves in a space— relating our size and perception of ourselves to the size of area we occupy? Where is our personal comfort zone? When it comes to the ability to move our bodies within a given space, people have differing abilities. One person has the balletic grace of a lithe dancer and can glide effortlessly in and through furniture lanes; another has the ungraceful navigation of a couch potato making zigzag tracks to the fridge. These two people cannot possibly relate in the same way to the same space. Their subliminal reactions to a room—the hard walls, the punctuations of natural light, and the obstacle course of furnishings—will vary widely.

Watch two different people furnish an identical room with the same furniture. How close do the walls feel? How close to the window must certain chairs be to prevent claustrophobia? How much room do you need to get around the coffee table? The organization and interpretation of space is not only a physical exercise; it is an emotional and personal one.

In my travels this is what I'm told: "Lynette, my room is too small. I can't use color, I can't use an 8-inch baseboard or a 6-inch crown molding, and my grandmother's hutch is too big." But this is what I hear: "My room feels too small."

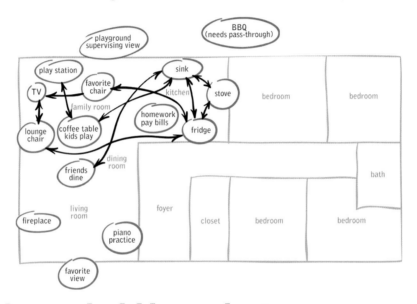

definition of household boundaries. STARTING WITH THE ROOM IN

WHICH YOU ARE SITTING, EVALUATE YOUR SPACE. Then ask every member of your household to evaluate or comment on the size and configuration of the room. Have each person do this individually, without the influence of the others' opinions. You might find that you all respond in the same way, at least to any obvious issues. Or you may be surprised at how differently each individual reacts to the room. This single but crucial evaluation of space and how you *feel* about that space will give you important clues to guide your decorating.

If, by the way, your reaction (or your household's collective reaction) is "way too small," and you feel that this lack of space is the crux of your decorating challenge, you're not alone. The overwhelming majority of people who come to me with decorating problems start with the complaint of too little space. Even those in 4,000-square-foot suburban homes complain: The rooms are too small or the wrong shape; the doors, windows, and fireplaces are awkwardly located.

First, let's identify space without numbers—no linear dimensions to describe the boundaries of a room. What is space to you? You might say, "The volume of air around me that's confined inside the walls of the room." That's only a fraction of the concept. Space is everything you can see, including very importantly what you see through the doorways and windows. So if the objective is to enlarge your space, you must take everything you see into consideration. Everything you see is your envelope of space. And every line, shape, or form within that visible area contributes to the interpretation of that space. How you organize those visuals—from the park outside your window to the arrangement of accessories on your mantel to the scale of your upholstery pattern—is how you make or break space.

You see that red rock mountain? It may not be on your property and you may not have deed or right-of-way. But it's yours—visually, anyway. Use it!

the no-nails, 7-step approach to getting a roomy feeling.

step 1 Take visual possession of all you can see.

If you can see it, it's yours to enjoy, manipulate, or ignore, whether it's over your lot line or not. Your visual space takes in all views on all sides. How you integrate that extended visual dimension into your area is important. There are many ways to do that. Here are tips to get you started:

Keep the imposition of window treatment on the glass area to a minimum, while still adding style and light/privacy control. Orienting furniture to the view isn't always necessary, but access is. Access is a key word. Access is the delicious ability to walk toward the view. A good example is a picture window or a bay window that you can walk up to. Think of any time you have been in a high-rise office building or an apartment twenty floors up or more. The first thing you do is walk to the window. When it's obstructed with furniture or draperies, your instinct is frustrated. How many times have you knelt on the sofa, leaned over its back, and parted the drapery to peer out the picture window? One of the reasons we love French doors is that they double as windows that signal approachability to the view. Besides the physical access, they give us subliminal access—the delicious possibility of instant contact with the outdoors.

In the wonderful Southwest home pictured here, the view is exceptional. The untreated window invites you to step up and survey the scene. The furniture arrangement centered in the room gives the fireplace and the view equal billing. Because the views are the art, walls are painted cream to serve as the mat of the picture.

I find that Southwest homes are decorated more in sync with their natural environment than anywhere else in the country. The colors of the indigenous red and yellow rock repeat here in the furnishings, rugs, and accessories, connecting the room to the outdoors. When interiors and the outdoors flow seamlessly into one another, it creates a "completeness" that makes the tiniest of homes feel expansive.

ABOVE: This is a delicious example of the connection of interior with exterior. A lovely shade tree, a container garden, and a brick walkway constitute a view just as important as a Rocky Mountain vista. It is intimate, colorful, relaxing, and full of line, depth, shape, and form. Whether it's on your property or your neighbors', in a high-density neighborhood or in farm country, work with whatever is in view. Bring it indoors and make it yours. In this case, the exterior has been drawn inside by the choice of building materials, as well as a nearly all-glass entry. Notice how the brick interior wall continues to the exterior walls as if it were a continuous original wall. The flooring materials also continue the texture, color, and pattern of the exterior walkway. You may not be able to match existing exterior materials with interior finishes, but you can blend the two with color and texture. Open your front or back doors. Look at the opportunities to bring the outdoors in with a new glass door and glass sidelights.

OPPOSITE: The focal point of this bedroom is the wall that includes a desk centered on the window and surrounded by built-ins. A simple window treatment—just enough for nighttime privacy—softens the transition between indoors and out, welcoming a view that includes a treed yard, dappled sunlight, and flowers. The quilt, accessories, and floral area rug all bring garden colors and patterns indoors. Would I object to white walls because there's no color? No, because the white is purposefully designed into the room. All the fabrics, floor covering, and accessories have white as a background, bringing a garden of flower colors forward. The room itself is doing the same thing on a larger scale: A white background sends all the color collectively forward, complementing the exterior inspiration. So why shutter the window behind the bed? This window probably looks onto the wall of the neighboring house. The shutters act as a backlit headboard and send your attention back to the view.

step 2 Minimize the impact of the window treatment on the window area. Mount

draperies so that as they stack to the sides, they just cover the trim molding and window casings. Sheers mask the view. Are they needed? All day? Can they be drawn back? Balloon shades and Roman shades need to be controlled. Less is more when you are trying to pull the outdoors in. Voluptuous balloon shades covering the top third of the window and stuffed with tissue paper are a double sin in this category: Not only do they obscure a third of the view area, but their bulk competes with the two-thirds of the view that is left!

Keep in mind that in addition to controlling light and privacy, draperies and curtains are there to soften the transition between the walls and the outside. Fabrics that are overly patterned or that contrast sharply with the wall color or the view become the center of attention and stop the eye from making a seamless transition from interior to exterior. Ease the eye to the exterior with window treatment choices that provide a transition rather than steal the scene.

A bedroom needs privacy, but isn't it wonderful to be able to wake to the morning sun and a view of a dappled backyard? Keep the window treatment under control. Simplify, and remember that it is merely a decorative transition between interior and exterior—not the main event.

step 3 Bring the view into the room with color!

One color-choice technique is to integrate the dominant colors of the view with those in the room. This isn't always possible, but if you have the opportunity to decorate around what you see outside, you might expand your space through color. If your view is a coniferous forest, for instance, or even a huge blue spruce in your front yard, a room colored in shades of evergreens and teals, from pastels to deeper hues, will bring the outdoors in. If your view is a cityscape dominated by the reds and yellows of brick and stone buildings, a warm color scheme will include them in your room space. On the other hand, if your view includes the house across the street with an orange front door and garage door that you abhor, don't use orange in your decor. The interior orange will draw your eye to the orange features across the street and emphasize the view you dislike. Rather, choose another element, such as a tree, for your indoor-outdoor connection. In a 36-story condo where sky is your view, pastels combined with cloud colors will expand the space. However, if you are never home during the day and city lights are your usual vista, darker, richer colors may work better for you. You see how personal the application of these techniques can be. The choice always depends on how you use your space and what you see.

Expand space with colors that let your eye dance between indoors and out. Here, a green ficus tree makes an instant interior-exterior connection.

step 4 Create long sight lines.

This is a trick I used in decorating model suites. Builders, of course, want rooms to look as large as possible. I used the concept of long sight lines. It works like this: As you approach a room and stand in the doorway, if you can see through to the baseboard at the farthest point, you have the impression of length and, subsequently, of space. Without that extended sight line, you may feel crowded out or blocked from entry. So, take a model-home lesson: Create furniture arrangements to allow a beeline of sight and movement from the entrance to the farthest point. Psychologically, this arrangement draws you into the room, and you can't help but step forward. The room feels comfortably spacious.

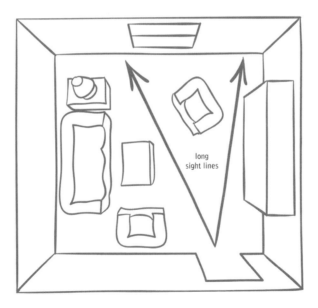

long
sight lines

ABOVE: From this doorway, you can see all the way to the baseboard across the room, so the space feels larger.

OPPOSITE: Placing a bed in the corner also can draw the eye to the farthest point in a room. When we experience a room, we tend to look at walls. When an object, an arrangement, or a focal point draws our attention to a corner, the room is extended. Angling a bed breaks up the boxy feeling common to small, square rooms.

step 5 Create furniture arrangements that are natural for activity and conversation.

Any seating arrangement larger than a square of 12×12 feet or 14×14 feet—what I call a conversational cluster—is too big for conversation. Beyond that distance, you would have to raise your voice to an impolite level.

While arranging your conversational cluster, turn your chairs slightly to send a message of invitation. Rigidly squared arrangements can be imposing, even forbidding; casually angled arrangements are more inviting. Do the party test: During the cleanup the next morning, notice how your closest friends have rearranged your furniture, the cushions, even the lamps or tables. These signs, subtle or obvious, will tell you how your room is supposed to work.

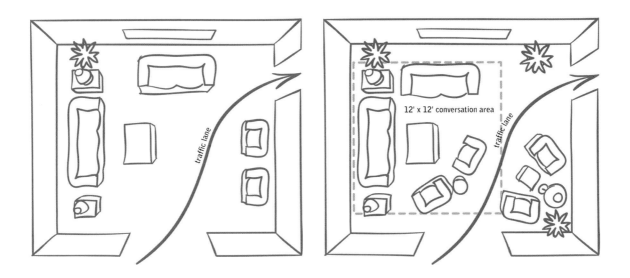

ABOVE LEFT: Although not large, this room is too big for one conversation cluster. ABOVE RIGHT: Anchored by an area rug, an intimate gathering of seating pieces is more inviting. Angling the chairs slightly enhances the welcoming feeling. The bonus? There's still room for a group of two friendly, face-to-face chairs in the corner! OPPOSITE: This room has exceptionally high ceilings and an overpowering fireplace. A traditional arrangement of a sofa perpendicular to the fireplace with chairs or another sofa opposite it would have made the fireplace the main event. But the main event would have been a big black hole topped with a high mantel dwarfing anyone seated nearby. The solution: Soften the impact of the imposing mantel with a soft, buttery yellow to absorb the contrast of the stone. And turn the fireplace into an elegant backdrop for the real main event: the conversation area. Pulled in from the walls, the seating pieces cluster as if drawn up to share a secret! This room says, "Won't you stay for tea? Let's chat."

Picture A. This is about as friendly and conducive to conversation as a waiting room!

If your room is larger than those conversational dimensions, don't stretch your arrangement or line the walls to fill the room. Instead, cluster conversation pieces comfortably and use the "extra" area for another grouping, a pair of comfortable chairs, a console table, or a writing desk. Even nothing more than a plant and art, photographs, or posters in a gallery arrangement can complete the space.

Here are two versions of the same room (shown above and opposite). Picture A is about as friendly and conducive to conversation as a waiting room! It looks as though you've pushed the furniture back for a dance or a Tupperware party. You can't get to the window to see out. One sofa has no access to the coffee table. Move the coffee table over to the sofa, and the problem reoccurs on the other side of the room. This is the most often made mistake in decorating: Pushing the furniture back to create a space that's not only unusable but uncomfortable and awkward.

Picture B. We've clustered the furniture for comfort and conversation.

In picture B we've closed up the space—used it! And what's interesting is that the room looks even more spacious. That's because the perception of space is created by the separation of the walls and furniture. You, too, can achieve a feeling of space around a sitting arrangement even if there is not much actual floor space. What do you do with the walls when there is no furniture to dress them? Nothing, because that nakedness is what makes the room feel spacious. When a room is not filled with stuff, there's space for something else—you! And that translates to a room that feels bigger than it really is.

THIS IS THE QUICKEST FIX IN THE ANNALS OF DECORATING. Make space by pulling the back of the sofa away from the wall by 6 to 10 inches! Sounds silly, but it works every time. Here's why: When you enter a room, you are confronted with shapes, light, color, and shadows. You take all of this in and process it into a single impression of space. When furniture lines the walls—especially if seating pieces are backed up to touch the walls—the subliminal message is one I call "the squeeze." The room feels tight. The solution is to loosen up to create shadows. Pulling the sofa away from the wall creates a 6- to 8-inch shadow. In that dark shadow, the distance between the sofa and the wall feels uncertain, sustaining the illusion of space.

ABOVE AND OPPOSITE: If your style is country, it's even more important to loosen up your furniture arrangements. After all, you chose this style for casual, friendly living. Pull your furniture around the view or the fireplace. Then deal with the rest of the room accordingly. If you have the space, create a second arrangement. But remember: Don't crowd the windows. This room is successful on several counts: It has an inviting conversation area. Although the walls are simply white, the room doesn't lack for color. The spunk is in the upholstery choices, but even they take second place to the collectibles. The fireplace was brought under control with a wash of white, which pulls it back into the wall color, so your eye goes to the accessories rather than focusing on an uninspiring brick hearth. And there's a wonderful bank of windows that you can walk along. Imagine the furniture parked against them instead—that would have been a design tragedy.

step 6 Don't crowd the entrance.

The entrance of the room is the "welcome zone." Watch newcomers enter your living room. Where do they pause or stop? If it's in the doorway, you may have an inadvertent crowding problem. Something may be sending an unwelcoming signal: "No room for you! Stand back."

Does this mean that you cannot back up a sofa and sofa table to the entry? No, that arrangement can work as long as the sofa is at a comfortable distance from the point of entry, and there is a clear path around it on either side.

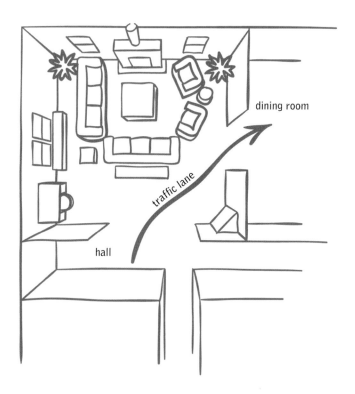

dining room

traffic lane

hall

ABOVE: Arrange furnishings so there is a clear pathway into the room.

OPPOSITE: In this living room, the parting of the chairs invites guests to walk in and settle on the down-filled sofa. The sofa also is pulled in from the back wall, allowing access to the inviting book-filled shelves behind it.

step 7 Look up.

Space is delicious. Too often, though, when we have it, we rush right out to buy more things to fill it up! One of the most common examples of this is the volumetric feature of a cathedral ceiling or lofted ceiling. There is always a two-story wall that goes with this common suburban-home feature. And with it comes a new homeowner whose first query is, *"What should I do with the big wall?"* The answer is...NOTHING! This is called negative space. Where there is nothing, the void says SPACE. If there is enough going on below that second-story space, your eye won't travel up. Ceiling volume is a wonderful feature, but you don't live up there! Its architectural purpose is to lift your subconscious and give you room to breathe. But high ceilings alone won't improve your sense of comfort if what is below that 8-foot "waterline" isn't working.

This master bedroom/sitting room presents an interesting challenge: high ceilings in adjoining medium-size rooms with a dividing privacy wall. Intimacy was the goal. Without the vertical paneling and heavy moldings the room would have felt too high and overscaled for its floor plan. A room like this in its original naked drywall-and-paint form is so very common, whether it's a bedroom (with or without the adjoining study) or even a living/dining room combination. Taking the color to the point where the ceiling breaks away from the wall and leaving the ceiling white would give the room a dunce's cap. Wallpaper also makes an unlikely solution unless the pattern is totally multidirectional. Whatever you choose for the walls should continue throughout the space. The key word here is space. This lofted area is what gives the room its space. That's why it is attractive to you. So leave it alone. Often I am asked how to decorate the end walls—the one or two vertical areas that reach to the peak. Do nothing, or add architectural elements: In this case, the ceiling area was emphasized by a deep and wide crown molding detail around the perimeter, giving the appearance of a recessed upper-wall area. Continuing the paneling on the end wall emphasizes the height and takes your eye up to the crossbeams. You want your eye to be drawn upward, but you don't want it to land on undressed walls. So use moldings and texture, all in the same colors. Notice how the walls and moldings, regardless of textural treatment, are cream and white.

furniture & accessories:
a balancing act

What makes some rooms so inviting? Why do others, even if handsome, feel uncomfortable? How you arrange your furnishings makes all the difference!

BALANCE. COMPOSITION. These words describe the interaction of elements that can turn a room into a comfortable space versus one that, even if handsome, may not encourage you to linger. As always, the furnishings and accessories you choose and how you arrange them is a very personal issue. **What do you need to make your home suit your lifestyle?** What sorts of arrangements—casual, formal, symmetrical, or delightfully off-kilter—**look balanced to your eye?**

Here's one way to increase your understanding of the concept of balance. Try this in your living room: Sit in each chair and on the sofa in each of the three positions. What do you see and how are you sitting? Straight or sidesaddle? Where does your eye naturally travel? What are you drawn to? Another test: **Everyone has a favorite chair, a favorite location in a room. Why?** Shouldn't all the chairs be comfortable? **Shouldn't every position have something beautiful to look at? A room is a collection of positions with views—and not just those views through a window.** A fireplace is a "view." A wall unit housing your favorite collection is a "view." So is a writing desk in the corner with a pretty vase of flowers from your garden (or the grocery) arranged with care by you. In designer language these are "focal points." But shouldn't every angle, every seat in the theater, have a focal point? **A room that achieves this is balanced.**

So often I see a lack of balance in a living room arrangement: sofa backed up against the picture window, matching end tables on either side, fireplace at the end of the room with a pair of chairs on either side. In all three sitting positions—on the sofa and in the two chairs beside the fireplace—everyone has to sit sidesaddle to see a focal point! And opposite the sofa is a traffic lane to an adjacent room.

Repeating materials and colors can create cohesiveness. White plus wood, in both the architectural details and in the furnishings, balance this setting.

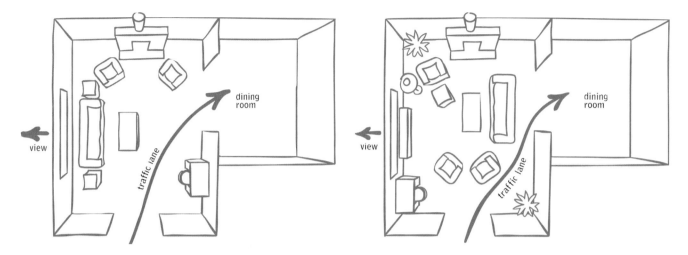

ABOVE: This sofa turns its back to the view. ABOVE RIGHT: With a little rearranging, furnishings can allow you enjoy both the fireplace and the view.

Take a look at the illustration, above left, to see what I mean. Now, look at the easy fix, above right. It only takes a bit of time to rearrange the furnishings so that the weighty sofa, fireplace, and view window are balanced—and everyone gets a view!

Let's consider that concept of balance again—this time applied to accessorizing one of the most important pieces of architectural real estate, the fireplace mantel. Balance is simply the arrangement of things in a way that feels good to you. For some, what feels right is a "papa-mama-baby bear" lineup of objects graduated in size. For others, only a symmetrical staging of pairs—an altar to the centered item—is acceptable. The third alternative is an asymmetrical arrangement of mixed-scale objects, a much looser and more forgiving approach that allows for continual trade-outs. And I suppose there is a fourth: a collection of trophies, old birthdays cards, dead mail, and keys!

Balance is not mathematical. It is the artistic placement of two or more items that complement each other in some way. It could be by size, shape, scale, color, or texture.

You may need to break a large room into two separate conversation groupings in order to focus on a fireplace at one wall and a view on the other.

They look well together. The yin and yang. But rather than worry that your arrangement may be incorrect, be assured that balance and composition are elements of art. If it's balanced to you, then it's balanced.

Just for fun, take a look at the two pictures below. They demonstrate various scales of items. Symmetrical or asymmetrical—which is more comfortable to you? Neither is incorrect. In the asymmetrical arrangement at left, a large mirror and a vase of flowers on one side balance the plates and mirror on the other. Does this look too loose for your own sensibilities? Then stick with the symmetry conveyed in the second photo where two matching lamps flank a painting.

ABOVE LEFT: Balance doesn't always mean symmetry. A loose, asymmetrical grouping creates a relaxed, friendly look.

ABOVE RIGHT: Some people aren't comfortable unless items are grouped with mirrorlike symmetry in mind. That's OK, too!

OPPOSITE: An oversize rooster struts his stuff in this kitchen. Balanced? Sure. The kitchen's gutsy elements, from rich woods to hefty ceiling beams and beefy clusters of baskets, almost demand a superlarge accent piece. Besides, it's fun.

12

clutter:
space enemy #1

Is your stuff squeezing you out of house and home? Clutter will fight that spacious feeling you've worked so hard to create. Here's help.

CLUTTER IS THE BIGGEST ENEMY OF SPACE. VISUAL CLUTTER CAN CONSIST OF TOO MANY accessories, too much furniture, too many pictures, plants, pillows, too many patterns—just too much of *anything*. If the eye has too much to take in, you feel as if your personal space has been absorbed. You feel pushed back toward the door, thinking, "No room for me," which translates to "This room is too small." Just as a palate cleanser in a fine meal gives the sense of taste a rest, your sense of sight needs a rest too. A barrage of line, shape, color, pattern, and form can be overwhelming.

This doesn't mean that a heavily decorated room is wrong. But what looks beautiful and what you can *live* with may not be the same. Continuous visual stimulation can make you crazy. At the opposite end of the clutter scale, contemporary austerity also can drive you mad! You've seen this technique in magazines, I'm sure: one Granny Smith apple on the end of a stark credenza against a naked taupe wall. Drop the mail on the other end, and you've destroyed the composition and the room. *Eeeeeiaaaaa!*

So let's get to the root of the problem. Here are just a few things that can shrink the feeling of space in a room: too much color contrast between large furniture pieces and the walls; over-patterned or overly bulky window treatments that obstruct or fight with the view; furniture placed around the perimeter or squeezed up against the walls giving the instant impression of a room that's too tight; furniture crowded toward the entrance of the room; clutter; poorly placed mirrors that double the confusion; too many small plants....Any of this sound familiar? Want to make a room seem bigger than it is? The answer is the KISS method: *Keep it Simple and Spacious!* In furniture choices, color, and placement of accessories, less is more.

This room proves that style and personality can go hand in hand with a serenely uncluttered scheme. With no busy fabrics and pattern to distract it, the eye can better appreciate the lines of the farm table and Windsor chairs, as well as the colors and textures of the charming but simple accessories.

It's often harder to decorate with restraint. **Limiting yourself to a few well-chosen pieces is the key.** But that takes time, thought, planning, and being brutally honest about the stuff you and your partner have been collecting. Paring down puts extra pressure on each item, how you place it, and the colors you choose. If you're just starting out, simplicity can reduce your initial investment, but it also means spending as much as you can on high-quality items and building decorative collections intelligently.

Why is it that at certain times of the year I want to clear off every shelf, mantel, and table surface, clean out the closets, and sort the basement and garage? I've never been able to connect this quirk to the change of seasons or the rhythms of my horoscope. It just happens, and when it does, I am positively dangerous. And yet, after the visual cacophony of Christmas, the de-treed living room feels disturbingly austere. When you live simply to begin with, it's easier to adjust your stuff to suit such changing moods.

Try this exercise. Place one object—a statue, for instance—in front of a blank wall, and let your eyes feast on every detail of the statue. Next, place a picture next to the statue so you have two objects—one three-dimensional and one two-dimensional—to take in; you've doubled the quantity of color, pattern, and scale. Now add a patterned wallpaper behind the two. Your attention is fractured; your brain is trying to decide which of these visuals is more important and what the total message is. Place these three elements in a room with 25 times more stuff and...!

The combination of traditional patterned furnishings, accessories, and collectibles creates a room that hovers on the edge of a visual cacophony. But not here! This room is a virtual flower garden. It works because a wall color pulled from one of the dominant colors in the upholstery fabric is also a driving color in the botanical prints. It's one of those outdoorsy neutrals that live in a real garden—a combination of foliage and earth that the eye takes for granted, even indoors in the context of floral motifs. The wall color is the grand organizer that sets off the white of the fireplace, the china, the mats on the pictures, even the embroidery on the cushions. Consistent color and mood are at work here.

show some restraint!
for big impact...keep it simple.

I love the subtle contrasts in this formal living room. Look at the walls: traditional provincial moldings and an ornate crown molding at the ceiling. And it's all one color—a contemporary shade of lichen green. Understated and calming. The wall moldings become texture. The fireplace mantel becomes art. The paintings, resting on the mantel instead of being hung, lend a friendliness to the room. Relaxed elegance. Against a dusted sage green wall, white furnishings could be austere—but not in this case: A raffia rug and a collection of mixed wood grains warm things up. The simplicity of the envelope, upholstery, and window treatment showcases a wide variety of collectibles without creating visual congestion.

lessons in looking.

SCALE. Scale refers to the relative size of objects or elements. Vary the scale to set things apart. In the scenarios on the opposite page, notice how different the scale of the accessories looks when the items are placed in front of patterned versus plain walls. Bring in the floral wallcovering, and the objects of affection are in danger of being absorbed into the wallcovering.

Look at the opposite page. In which photos do the objects stand out and appear bolder? In the examples showing the teapots and ladies, note how the objects virtually disappear when placed in front of a floral wallpaper that has a pattern of exactly the same scale as the flowers on the accessories, above left. Seen from across the room, this collection would be completely lost. Now note how much easier it is to see the pieces against a plain green wall, below left.

In the pitcher-and-plate combination, above right, the objects seem bigger and bolder when viewed against the plain, painted wall. However, the larger scale of the objects, the boldness of their shapes, and the addition of some solid colors save this grouping from being swallowed up by the floral wall pattern, below right. Using these lessons, you can begin to figure out if the objects you love are getting the attention they deserve in your home.

Patterned accessories stand out against solid-color walls, but they virtually disappear when placed in front of wallpaper with the same-scale pattern.

EMPHASIS. An object's placement and how it is positioned to relate to other items in a grouping can force someone to look at it—or not.

For instance, in the picture at top left, you see the wonderful turn of the vase. It looks like an important piece. (Actually $4.95 at a discount store!) However, in the picture at top right, the eye is compromised: The vase is beautiful, but now the eye must try to to enjoy two distinct items. Actually, these look good together because one is three-dimensional and the other is more on the order of flat art. But they are now of equal importance. Place a patterned wallpaper behind them, as shown in the picture on the bottom, and they change again: The vase once again comes forward, the picture is absorbed into the background.

Clutter takes energy to live with—and not just for cleaning and maintenance. For some, visual stimulation boosts adrenaline; for others, it instigates a headache. Again, a personal issue. Consider these suggestions as you purchase and arrange your stuff. Get it together: For example, rather than letting a frog collection hop all over the house (and drag your eye around with it), group the frogs in one place where your eye can stop and rest. Think big: When it comes to plants, one larger tropical plant does much more for a room than a forest of $2.99 specials. It becomes an architectural element and draws the outside in. And if your problem is just too much of everything, have a garage sale and use the proceeds toward that cruise you've dreamed of taking!

COMPOSITION. There is no "right" or "wrong" way to arrange objects. As with organizing your space or choosing your colors, it's all up to what works for your eye. Some people prefer an exacting order that would make others nervous and uptight. For example, some people inevitably arrange objects in "papa-mama-baby-bear"

ABOVE: To emphasize a well-loved piece, let it stand alone. ABOVE RIGHT: Paired with a picture of equal weight, this vase loses half of its importance.

ABOVE: A patterned wallpaper swallows up the picture and puts the pattern-free vase centerstage again.

descending order, as shown at top left. Others need a looser, random arrangement in which asymmetrical clusters of objects balance each other, as shown in the photos at top right, below left, and below right. Try these arrangements on the opposite page with three of your favorite objects and see what feels right to you.

CONSOLIDATION. Consolidation is another solution to clutter. Look at the mantels below: Four objects equally spaced use up all of the placement area yet provide no focus for the eye. Nested into tighter compositions, the same objects on the second mantel leave open areas that communicate space and give your eye a resting spot.

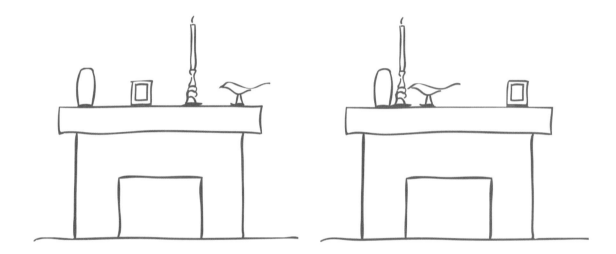

ABOVE LEFT: Objects set in descending order may seem orderly to some or staid to others. ABOVE RIGHT: Clusters of overlapping objects please the eye.

ABOVE LEFT AND ABOVE RIGHT: Use these composition examples as you arrange some of your favorite objects on a mantel, hall table, or dresser.

double trouble

13

Mirror, mirror on the wall....
Before you hang a framed mirror or, trickier yet,
decide to mirror an entire wall,
heed these tips and warnings—and make sure
that the mirror will reflect something
that's worth a second look.

MORE DECORATING SINS ARE COMMITTED WITH MIRROR THAN WITH ANY OTHER DECORATIVE MATERIAL. Most of the complaints I hear are from those who thought mirrors would solve their decorating problems. After spending a great deal of money (and destroying their drywall during installation), they end up hating the result. Why?

Write 500 times: "Mirrors double everything! Mirrors double everything...."

Before you hang mirrors, consider what they will reflect. I've seen living rooms given the uninviting look of hotel lobbies by mirror that visually doubles the seating area. Two staircases get you a grand ballroom; double fireplaces, a mountain lodge. The one I've never understood is mirroring the kitchen backsplash. I have enough trouble with a messy kitchen without doubling the clutter. While I continue to believe that whatever is right for *you* is all right, how about a few tips?

Mirrors expand space only when they reflect a spatial element. Double a view through a window, reflect an adjacent wall to visually lengthen a room, **or create an image of infinity by reflecting a corner where two walls come together.** As for reflecting furniture, you almost need to under-furnish a room to counteract mirror's doubling effect.

Enlarging a room with mirrors means creating an optical illusion, stretching the room's apparent dimensions. That illusion occurs when plate mirror installed wall-to-wall and floor-to-ceiling creates a continuous plane; by illusion the wall doubles in length. Applied to the wall, plate mirror should extend to the intersection of the adjacent wall—tight to the corner with no frame. It should also continue to the ceiling and to the floor, which means removing both the crown molding and the baseboard, so that the ceiling and floor planes look continuous as well. If you stop the mirror at

Mirrors work well when you want to punch a hole in a wall—figuratively speaking, that is. Here, the oversize mirror, balanced by the width of the pine bench below it, reflects the large picture window across the room, giving a once-dull hallway a newfound view.

the baseboard, you will make it appear that you must step over the baseboard to walk into the extension of the room. Here are some tips for plate mirror: In a foyer, mirror a wall that is perpendicular to the door. In a living room, mirror a wall opposite a large window. In bedrooms, a mirror on the headboard will double the bed and crowd the room, so reflect the window view, instead. Dining rooms make wonderful candidates for mirrors, because they are essentially a stage with four background walls. In bathrooms, be careful not to reflect the underworkings of toilets and pedestal sinks.

Like an exquisite crystal chandelier, the sparkle of a mirror is mesmerizing. Accessorizing with large framed mirrors adds space as well as sparkle. One smaller mirror, in a group of pictures or tucked into the niche of a lamp-centered still life is a stunning accessory. As a backdrop for plants and floral arrangements, mirrors double your investment. *Proceed with caution.*

ABOVE: Mirror came to the rescue of these closet doors. What was once a drab anteroom/closet to a very small bedroom is now a boudoir, thanks to the installation of mirror in the doors' recessed panels.

OPPOSITE: In this traditional bedroom, the mirror area is obscured by the objects and their reflections. The mirror provides glitter and a gilded frame, an important anchor in this composition.

14

psst...this is personal

THIS IS THE SHORTEST CHAPTER OF ALL—BECAUSE YOU HAVE TO WRITE THE REST OF IT YOURSELF! Decorating your home may not be easy, but it is fun. *Even self-indulgent.* That's because the process encourages—no, *requires*—that you stop and think about yourself for a change. Who are you? What do you like? How do you want to live? What kind of stuff do you want to live with? *Cool, eh?*

By explaining the design basics in this book, I have put tools in your hand. Tools, not rules. In the end, good design is all about freedom—to do things your way, to forget fads (or what your neighbors think). *It's your home, for heaven's sake.*

Decorating requires that you stop and think about who

Let's see now...Where to begin? How about creating a scheme around the colors you've always loved? Or rearranging your living room to accommodate that hobby you've never had space for? Or carving out space in your bedroom for the comfy chaise that you've been coveting for years? Or...(*you fill in the blank!*)...?

Lynette Jennings

you are and how you want to live.

index

A
Accent colors, 166, 168, 170–173
Access, to views, 186, 200
Accessories
  arranging, 224–227
  balancing, 210, 212, 213
  scale and, 222–223
  uncluttered, 218, 224
Art, contemporary, 16–17, 60
Art plates, 16–17
Asymmetrical arrangements, 212

B
Balance, 208–213
Bathrooms, light and color in, 90, 92, 138, 158
Bauhaus style, 52
Bedrooms
  casual, 18–19
  color in, 84, 98, 100, 110, 158, 159, 168
  high ceilings in, 204–205
  maximizing space in, 188–189, 94–195
  mirrors in, 232, 233
  on porches, 26–27
  window treatments for, 188–189, 190–191
Beige, 84–88, 154, 156, 170–171
Black, 136–139
Built-ins, 172–173, 189

C
Ceiling beams, 154–155
Ceilings, high, 197, 204–205
Checks, 177
Children, activity spaces for, 30, 54
Clutter, 216–221, 224
Color charting system, 128–134
Colors
  accent, 166, 168, 170–173
  in bathrooms, 90, 92, 138, 158
  in bedrooms, 84, 98, 100, 110, 158, 159, 168
  beige, 84–88, 154, 156, 170–171
  breaking "rules" of, 32, 74, 80
  brilliant, 162–163
  charting system, 128–134
  choosing, 118–134
  confidence with, 71, 74, 76–77, 88, 92, 104–106, 111, 166–170
  cool, 107–108, 150–151
  dark, 136–139
  in dining rooms, 68–69, 75, 76–77, 98, 99, 111, 163
  of dirt,148-149
  effects of, 70–71, 74
  exterior inspirations, 140-151
  furniture and, 94–98, 100–102
  in guest rooms, 83–84
  home sales and, 109–110
  in kitchens, 32–33, 35, 95, 96, 101, 138–139, 168, 178–179
  light and, 90–92, 106–109, 146–148, 150–151, 158, 159
  in living rooms, 87, 137, 142–143, 155, 169, 176–177
  monochromatic schemes, 13, 154–155, 170–171
  natural, 147–149, 164–165
  neutral, 85–89, 154, 156, 158, 159, 219
  Northeast, 146–147, 150–151
  open plans and, 102–104, 123
  perception of, 114–116, 124–125
  on porches, 165
  purple, 34–35, 72–73, 162–163, 174–175
  red, 135, 170–171
  for small rooms, 83–86, 88–89, 96, 192–193
  Southwest, 141–146
  white, 82, 101–102, 154–159, 188–189
  window treatments and, 99, 109
  wood and, 94–98, 100–102, 157
  yellow, 176–177
Consolidation, 226–227
Contemporary style, 16–17, 52–63, 75
Conversation clusters, 196–200
Country style, 72–73, 200–201

D
Deconstructionism, 42
Decorating myths, 80–111
Design
  freedom in, 28–34, 236
  process of, 20–21, 24–25, 66
Dining rooms
  color in, 68–69, 75, 76–77, 98, 99, 111, 163
  contemporary-style, 16–17, 60–61, 75
  country-style, 72–73
  mirrors in, 232
  simplicity in, 216–217

E
Easy elegance, 13
Eclecticism, 42, 59
Entrances, maximizing space in, 202

F
Fabrics, color and, 120, 122–127, 131–135, 171
Fiestaware, 168
Fireplaces, 196–197, 200–201, 210, 211, 220–221
Flow, 130
Freedom, in decorating, 28–34, 236
Furniture
  arranging, 186–187, 194–203, 208–213
  large-scale, 94–98
  naturalistic, 52
  nontraditional uses for, 26–27, 28, 29, 30–31

acknowledgments
Special thanks to photographers Bill Holt,
Emily Minton, and John Haigwood.